The Agile Leader:
Navigating Change and Uncertainty with Agility

By: Mustafa Nejem

Table of Contents

Chapter **1**

Introduction to Agile Leadership

1.1 What is agile leadership?:

Leaders today face increasing complexity, uncertainty and rapid change. The world is changing faster than ever before and success requires the ability to adapt quickly. However, most leadership models are still based on principles of stability, control and planning for the predictable future. This mismatch has left many leaders struggling with how to effectively navigate today's VUCA world.

Agile leadership provides a new leadership paradigm focused on embracing change, building resilience and fostering innovation. At its core, agile leadership is about developing the skills and mindsets needed to thrive amid uncertainty. It emphasizes adapting to changing external realities rather than attempting to exert rigid control. Agility allows leaders and their organizations to respond proactively to opportunities and challenges as they emerge.

Agile leadership draws from concepts in agile project management, which focuses on iterative development, rapid adaptation and continuous improvement. However, rather than only applying to teams executing projects, agile principles must permeate the entire organization from top to bottom. It requires a cultural shift towards experimentation, learning and ever-evolving strategies and solutions.

The term "agile" refers to being able to move quickly and easily. This may seem counterintuitive when applied to large organizations, which are often associated with bureaucracy and inertia. However, agility is not about reacting hastily without planning or thought. Rather, it is the skillful and strategic application of a flexible, learning-focused approach.

Some key principles of agile leadership include:

Rapidly adapting strategies and plans based on ongoing learning and changing realities rather than rigidly sticking to obsolete preconceived notions.

Fostering a culture of innovation where creativity and experimentation are rewarded. New ideas are turned into action through iterative development and testing.

Distributing leadership throughout self-organizing teams utilizing diverse perspectives and expertise from all levels.

Quickly responding to market signals and disruptions by reconfiguring resources and capabilities as needed rather than maintaining static structures.

Traditional leadership models emphasize meticulous long-term planning and maintaining control. However, in today's fast-paced business environment, preconceived strategic plans often become quickly outdated. Attempting to exert control over unpredictable external conditions can also be counterproductive.

Agile leadership takes a different approach centered around curiosity, autonomy and adaptability rather than control. Leaders adopt the mindset of a learner continually refining their understanding rather than assuming they have all the answers upfront. Continuously challenging underlying assumptions allows for new perspectives to emerge from within teams.

Rather than a reliance on detailed planning, agile leaders focus on establishing a clear overall vision and set of values to guide autonomous, self-organizing teams. Teams are then empowered to experiment with different approaches for accomplishing goals using their expertise and insights from iterative learning. This distributed, empowered model of leadership fosters innovation by leveraging the collective intelligence of all individuals.

Strategies are developed experimentally through rapid prototyping rather than meticulous planning cycles. Minimum viable products are tested with real customers as early as possible to gather feedback to refine the approach. Rolled out incrementally, solutions quickly evolve based on ongoing learning rather than large speculative investments predicted on static assumptions.

By developing an ability to rapidly learn and pivot as needed, agile organizations build resilience to survive unforeseen changes. An experimental mindset also helps proactively shape the future through innovative new offerings rather than just reacting to disruptions.

Traditional command-and-control styles of leadership tend to value stability and adhering to plans above all else. However, in a volatile environment, rigidly sticking to outdated assumptions can be devastating. Agile leaders understand that strategies and solutions must be continuously evaluated and refreshed based on what is working now rather than clinging to what was planned in the past.

Rather than viewing failure or changes as problems to be avoided, agile organizations see them as opportunities to learn. Failures from experiments provide valuable performance data to inform iterative improvements. New insights from disruptions are leveraged to strengthen capabilities and open up new market opportunities. An experimental culture where it is safe to fail facilitates continuous progress towards what works best over time.

While planning has its place, traditional leaders often get mired developing exhaustive plans for every possible scenario. For volatile conditions, extensive planning mainly serves to instill a false sense of control and predictability. Agile leadership focuses on establishing clearly defined goals and values to guide rapid decision making with imperfect information. Teams are empowered to continually learn through improvisation, adapting strategies along the way rather than rigidly executing preconceived plans.

By developing skills like rapid learning, resilience, flexibility and innovation, agile leadership cultivates an organizational culture wired for success amid uncertainty rather than just stability and control.

Agile leadership represents a paradigm shift away from command-and-control models of leadership unsuited for today's VUCA world. Rather than striving to exert rigid control over changing environments, agile leaders foster cultures defined by empowerment, adaptability, innovation and resilience.

Through distributing leadership, agile leaders empower high-performing teams to self-organize around a shared vision and drive experimental progress autonomously. Strategies are developed iteratively through rapid prototyping cycles that leverage continuous feedback to inform high-quality, just-in-time solutions.

By developing an agile mindset, organizations build an inherent ability to both shape disruptive change and endure unforeseen changes. An emphasis on rapid learning allows ongoing refinement of strategies based on emerging realities rather than adherence to outdated assumptions.

While planning has its place, agile leadership values emerging opportunities from failures and disruptions over exhaustive preconceived plans. Responsiveness, adaptation and innovation become core competencies that strengthen competitive advantage in dynamic conditions.

In this chapter, we will explore agile leadership concepts and principles in more depth. Upcoming sections will provide examples of agile leaders, examine how to cultivate key agile mindsets and discuss strategies for nurturing an agile culture.

1.2 Why agile leadership matters today

The business landscape has never experienced change at the pace and scale occurring today. Emerging technologies, shifting customer preferences and global disruptions introduce unprecedented levels of uncertainty. As a result, leadership skills focused on stability such as detailed planning are increasingly mismatched for this new reality.

Today's economy demands agility to both ride the waves of ongoing transformation and shape the future proactively through innovation. Leaders must cultivate an organizational mindset adapted for the unknown if they hope to compete amid volatility. Research shows that over 75% of S&P 500 firms from the 1950s are now gone due to an inability to renew business strategies.

With change happening exponentially faster, the half-life of skills is decreasing along with the expiration date of strategic plans. Rigidity has become a liability as disruptive startups continuously reshape industry norms. Legacy giants struggle competing with new nimble entrants unencumbered by inertia from past successes. As a result, today more than ever agility provides a competitive advantage.

For businesses, the opportunity cost of failing to adjust strategies quickly enough is lost market share, irrelevance or even failure. For individuals, an inability to rapidly develop new skills leaves many vulnerable to disruption. Leaders must foster ongoing learning to help organizations and employees thrive amid uncertainty rather than just survive changes. Agile problem-solving abilities are increasingly mission critical talent requirements.

While disruptive changes pose threats, they also create new opportunities that agile organizations are positioned to capture. Traditional markets are being reshaped by evolving customer expectations around environmental sustainability, experiences and well-being. Leaders embracing agility can proactively drive innovation to meet the demands of these new experience economies.

For example, legacy retailers disrupted by e-commerce saw growth opportunities by reinventing physical spaces as community hubs. Companies developing plant-based alternatives gained market share from health-conscious consumers. As work becomes distributed, new platforms empowering flexible work arrangements gain traction. Agile leaders scan the horizon for weak signals of shifting priorities to get ahead of curves.

In contrast, lack of agility leaves organizations vulnerable. Static strategies focused on preserving the past rather than shaping the future risk missing inflection points. Lacking innovation avenues, businesses stagnate as needs outpace outdated offerings. Silos prioritizing their piece of the pie over collaborative ideation stifle emergence of new solutions.

Rigidity also takes an organizational toll. Inability to adapt strategies dampens morale as realities diverge from obsolete plans. Individual contributors stuck executing outmoded processes lose engagement. Ultimately, lack of agility spells doom as change accelerates and competitors seize opportunities neglected through inertia.

Embracing agility helps organizations remain aligned and energized amid flux. Continuous experimentation keeps the focus on emerging realities rather than theoretical plans. Cross-functional collaboration sparks novel ideas by blending diverse expertise. Iterative learning cycles propel solutions forward adaptively rather than betting big on predictions.

Agile organizations enjoy competitive advantages like increased innovation, greater strategic flexibility, and higher morale. By cultivating an experimental culture, leaders tap into a network effect where each new idea builds on those before. 3M famously generated over $926 million in annual revenues from products launched within the last five years, keeping their portfolio fresh.

Netflix also exemplifies the power of agility. By continuously refining their platform based on usage data, they identified underserved niches like international expansion. Instead of rigidly defending legacy DVD rentals, they pioneered cloud-based streaming—a disruptive innovation that doomed Blockbuster's static strategies.

Leaders embracing agility gain flexibility to reconfigure resources as conditions evolve rather than committing to rigid structures. Spotify survived the download era by pivoting sales models to subscriptions when streaming emerged. Toyota thrives through its ability-focused factories, reconfiguring production swiftly to adjust to parts shortages or new models.

Studies also link agility to higher employee engagement. Empowered teams energized by mission and purpose find work more meaningful than just executing predetermined plans. Turnover decreases as people grow skills through diverse challenges rather than stagnating in narrow roles. Morale strengthens organizations' ability to endure challenges as turbulent changes disrupt rigid peers.

Overall, agility arms leaders with competitive tools like perpetual innovation, strategic versatility and high-engagement culture—equipping businesses for VUCA environments where change is constant. The next submission will provide leadership examples demonstrating agile mindsets.

Certain leaders have exemplified agile mindsets through approaches like experimentation, resilience, and distributed leadership. Jeff Bezos transformed Amazon into an innovation juggernaut through a culture of rapid testing and willingness to fail. At Amazon, new products like the Kindle reader and web services introduced major strategic shifts—achieved through thousands of experiments annually.

Alibaba's Jack Ma also empowers rapid learning cycles. Ma believes success stems not from perfection, but exploring 10,000 approaches to identify the 1 that works best. Under his leadership, Alibaba incubated disruptive innovations like Alipay by trying ideas iteratively at low-cost rather than extensive planning.

Indra Nooyi demonstrated resilience leading PepsiCo's strategic shift towards health-focused brands amid sugar backlash. By scanning weak signals, she recognized changing consumer values early and smoothly transitioned PepsiCo's portfolio through initiatives like reduction of saturated fat and sugar. Her agility protected market share.

Richard Branson cultivates innovation by valuing diversity of perspective. The Virgin Group's decentralized approach taps unconventional thinkers, incubating disruptors like Virgin Galactic through autonomous subsidiaries. Branson inspires radicals able to challenge status quo assumptions fueling new ventures.

These leaders point to competitive advantages unlocked through agility-drivers like embracing experimentation, anticipating weak signals, empowering diverse ideas, and accepting imperfection as a learning tool. The next submission will further illustrate benefits to individuals and organizations of cultivating agile mindsets.

Agile leadership is increasingly critical for navigating today's business landscape defined by uncertainty and disruption at an unprecedented scale. Traditional leadership strategies reliant on meticulous planning and control are mismatched for constant change characteristic of VUCA environments.

Challenges facing leaders lacking agility include inability to renew strategies quickly enough to keep pace with evolution. Outdated assumptions and rigid structures also stifle innovation needed to shape the future proactively. Over-commitment to past successes breeds inertia disabling reinvention.

In contrast, organizations embracing principles of agility unlock competitive advantages. An experimental culture stimulates perpetual innovation, strengthening alignment with shifting customer demands. Distributed leadership and empowered teams foster strategic flexibility to reconfigure nimbly. Iterative learning strengthens resilience, maintaining morale and focus amid flux.

Exemplar leaders demonstrate mindsets facilitating reinvention through approaches like valuing failure as feedback, decentralizing decision making, future-scanning for weak signals, and questioning assumptions. Their successes point to individual, team and organizational benefits of cultivating agility as a strategic competency.

Agile leadership has never been more vital given today's VUCA realities. The following sections will delve deeper into strategies for developing key agile mindsets as a foundation for sustainable reinvention and competitiveness.

1.3 Change and uncertainty as the new normal

The half-life of skills is rapidly decreasing due to constant industry disruptions. What was previously considered a long-term career is now more akin to an iterative journey of perpetual learning and reinvention. Gone are the days where stability reigned and 5-year plans stretched far into the foreseeable future. Today, leading amid constant change requires an agile mindset grounded in three overarching realities:

Weak signals pointing to major disruptions emerge years ahead but are easy to miss. Technology breakthroughs like mobile internet or decentralized ledgers lay dormant for years before mainstream impact. Agile leaders develop skills to detect anomalies amid noise indicating paradigm shifts.

The exponential pace of technological progress compounds uncertainty. Emerging innovations like AI, robotics and biotechnology are reshaping entire industries far faster than previous industrial revolutions through compound growth. Leaders must progress agile thinking commensurate with acceleration.

A diversity of perspectives is key to strategic adaptability. As conditions evolve, those embedded in the status quo are often the last to recognize implications. Agile leaders foster viewpoints from diverse demographics attuned to subtle shifts leaders may overlook.

To succeed amid perpetual change, organizations must develop an agility muscle memory at both the senior leadership level along with all employees. This concluding part will examine how leaders can nurture an agile state of mindset organizationally.

Identifying weak signals early allows agile leaders to get ahead of major changes rather than just reacting to disruptions. Google pioneered search ads by noticing minor anomalies in keyword search patterns pointing toward untapped monetization. Had they ignored oddities, others would have disrupted their core business.

Likewise, researchers note weak signals preceded past disruptions, including mobile internet keywords in 2002 and early mentions of "Facebook" replacing Myspace in 2005. Agile thinking involves rigorously analyzing emerging utilization patterns and minor anomalies for clues of potential inflection points.

Exponential technologies also demand constant skill progression. What seems implausible today like disease cures or AI assistance may seem commonplace in just years due to doubling effects. Leaders must instill a culture where every person is always learning to rapidly develop new competencies.

For instance, Toyota cultivates learning agility through its "Point Zero" program inspiring ideas to help factories leverage emerging tech. Similarly, Anthropic trains AI researchers through micro-credentialing so ideas proven implausible today become part of skillsets tomorrow. Incremental, lifelong comprehension builds resilience.

Finally, diversity of thought counters blind spots from conformity. Disruptions often resonate earliest with those on the periphery seeing different contexts leadership may miss. Coinbase fosters varied perspectives through programs facilitating global exposure and meritocracy over pedigree.

Such efforts counter biases threatening adaptability by welcoming subtle signals affecting minority populations first before becoming mainstream changes. An inclusive culture strengthens situational awareness needed for agile strategizing.

As the challenges of exponential change grow, developing a growth mindset becomes ever more crucial for individuals and organizations alike. Leaders must cultivate an environment where no one feels content in their current abilities, and all are driven to expand competencies constantly.

Netflix exemplifies this through initiatives like their "Jedi Council" convening top performers regularly to hone problem-solving talents. At Google, 20% of employee time is devoted to passion projects stimulating new skills. Such efforts continuously push boundaries of existing knowledge through self-driven learning.

Agile leaders also encourage prudent risk-taking and learning from failures. 3M's experimental model cultivates thousands of ambitious projects annually, accepting many will fail but fueling a portfolio of disruptors. Likewise, Anthropic frames AI safety research as a journey where dead-ends accelerate progress more than predetermined solutions.

To survive accelerating changes, resilience must also be strengthened organizationally. Toyota preaches "building people before building cars" through cross-training yielding flexibility. At Autodesk, retraining programs reassure those disrupted there are roles, weakening impacts of transformations on morale.

Taken together, proactively developing capacities for learning, experimenting, failing safely and quickly recovering from disruptions outfit individuals and groups for a future demanding perpetual agility. However, nurturing such mindsets requires sincere buy-in from leadership. The realities of constant technological progress, weak signals emerging years ahead of disruptions, and diversity as a strategic asset require agile thinking as the new normal for sustainable success. Leaders must cultivate an organizational culture and mindsets adaptive to this age of perpetual change.

Exemplar companies demonstrate strategies for building agility at scale. Developing a growth mindset through initiatives like passion projects and cross-training pipelines individuals and teams for reinvention. Encouraging prudent risk-taking and learning from failures on a large yet controlled scale spurs unconventional solutions.

Proactively reskilling and redeploying the workforce builds resilience against transitions otherwise threatening stability. Framing disruptions collaboratively as opportunities gathering diverse inputs counters conformity risks from the status quo.

As uncertainty becomes the only constant, nurturing everyday agility necessitates moving beyond reaction to shaping the future proactively. Leaders able to establish conditions where individuals and organizations consistently challenge assumptions and expand competencies will endure what may defeat rigid peers. The next chapter section will drill into strategies for cultivating key aspects of an agile mindset.

Chapter 2
Embracing Change and Adapting Quickly

2.1 Developing a growth mindset

Embracing change begins with cultivating a growth mindset seeing potential in every circumstance rather than limitations. As economist Joseph Schumpeter recognized, 'Creative Destruction' fuels prosperity by replacing outdated practices with innovative alternatives. However, this means transitions are constant and skills renewal perpetual for individuals and businesses alike. Developing a learning orientation becomes vital for thriving amid disruption.

Pioneering research by Carol Dweck revealed fixed and growth mindsets impacting achievement. Those with fixed perspectives see skills as inherent traits rather than cultivated talents. Struggles imply deficits vs. opportunities. Conversely, growth-oriented individuals welcome challenges through a belief that effort shapes abilities over time.

Cultivating this outlook strengthens agility by instilling confidence that emerging demands can be met through diligence. Leaders able to diffuse instability by role-modelling lifelong curiosity will inspire reinvention necessary for sustainable success. Three practices central to growth mindset development include:

1. Reframing failures as valuable lessons
2. Celebrating the process as rewards
3. Framing criticism as useful feedback

Cultivating these behaviors at scale reshapes perceptions of change from adversities into advantages. The following sections will discuss techniques for operationalizing this orientation organizationally.

Reframing failures as learning experiences strengthens resilience against setbacks inevitable amid change. Leaders demonstrate this by transparently sharing mistakes and lessons learned. For example, at Anthropic research briefs analyze theories disproven to spare others wasted paths.

Acknowledging imperfections also lifts reluctance to innovative risks. 3M famously protected experimentation through a "15% rule" letting scientists explore hunches 15% of work time. Thousands of attempts annually fueled disruptors like post-it notes despite many failures.

Success stories likewise celebrate incremental progress rather than perfect endings. Netflix highlights struggles developing authentication before streaming gained traction. Highlighting iterative advances honors small wins fueling disruptors, motivating teams facing setbacks.

Leaders also showcase growth through difficult feedback. Branson discusses criticisms shaping Virgin into an agile innovator. Appraisals focus on tailoring strengths and stretching limited skills rather than deficiencies. Conveyed non-judgmentally, this lifts potential through guided self-improvement.

Regularly sharing missteps, works-in-progress and development areas models growth while mitigating stigma hindering change. Over time, it establishes beliefs that skills evolve daily through experiential learning rather than innate talents.

Fostering a growth mindset also involves establishing an environment where skills development is a priority for all. Netflix cultivates this by allocating 20% of employee time to skill-building. 3M invests over $1 billion annually ensuring its 80,000+ staff continually expand competencies.

Likewise, Anthropic provides micro-credentials incentivizing continual mastery of adjacent disciplines. Toyota cross-trains factory workers across processes to strengthen versatility. Mandating ongoing enrichment through such initiatives treats learning as core to each role.

Mentorship additionally nourishes growth by empowering staffers to shape their journeys. At 18F, junior employees lead projects while seasoned advisors provide support tailored to strengths. Fostering autonomy balanced with guidance nurtures perseverance through challenges.

Reverse-mentoring likewise disrupts limitations as seniors share knowledge with juniors. Exposure to fresh perspectives broadens outlooks while deepening cultural sensitivities. It breaks assumptions that skills follow titles or years of experience alone.

Taken together, role-modelling resilience transparently; prioritizing continual skills expansion through initiatives like cross-training and micro-credentials; and leveraging mentorship to empower self-directed advancement cultivates a learning mindset organizational DNA.

Reward systems must also reinforce efforts and persistence and not just results alone. LinkedIn recognition programs spotlight contributions strengthening networks versus only quotas met. Peer spot bonuses at Anthropic spotlight cooperation showcasing its cultural importance.

Praise also acknowledges small wins fueling progress over immediate achievements. Relaying near-miss failures treats attempts constructively rather than as wasted resources. Progress updates focus on capabilities developed and new ideas emerging from unconventional approaches.

Strategic messaging frames changes positively as opportunities rather than adversities too. Patagonia conveys layoffs not as cost-cutting but new challenges to innovate sustainable growth. Reinforcing transformations as advantages reshapes perceptions of disruption organizationally.

Leaders engage staff directly to diffuse uncertainty. All-hands discussions by the C-Suite acknowledge unease but share renewed purpose and confidence in abilities to rise together. Calls highlighting common ground over differences fosters cohesion amid flux.

Instilling perceptions that disruptions yield prospects prepares mindsets for reinvention. With resilience and collegial support, settlements smooth otherwise difficult transition conclusion, cultivating a growth mindset through deliberate techniques strengthens agility amid constant change. Role-modelling resilience and sharing setbacks transparently mitigates perspectives seeing abilities as innate vs cultivated talents. Prioritizing continual skills expansion through initiatives like cross-training and micro-credentials reinforces beliefs that competencies evolve daily.

Leveraging mentorship empowers self-directed learning and dispersing wisdom across levels disrupts limitations. Framing recognition, rewards and communications positively highlights small wins, efforts and opportunities inherent to disruptions. Combined, these strategies instill perseverance and confidence that emerging demands can be met through diligence.

Exemplar companies demonstrate growth mindset proliferation creates an environment where reinvention is a cultural norm rather than an adverse reaction. Individuals thriving on challenges become empowered change agents, while organizations welcome flux as fuels of progress.

The next chapter will explore strategies for fostering a culture embracing prudent risk-taking and experimentation to strengthen innovativeness amid constant change. This establishes leadership skills enabling forward-looking adaptability as the status quo rapidly evolves.

2.2 Responding proactively to change signals

While a growth mindset embraces change, agile leadership means anticipating transformations rather than just reacting to disruptions. Subtle signals frequently arise years ahead of coming shifts, but recognition demands situational awareness. Leaders must develop proactive scanning abilities to identify weak indicators and channel uncertainty into opportunity.

Futurist Paul Saffo notes emerging patterns often reside "on the periphery" attracting minority interests before breakthroughs reconstitute industries. Staying sharply attuned allows leadership pursuing disruptions rather than passively awaiting their arrival. Three strategies central to responsive scanning involve:

1. Broadening information sources
2. An Analyzing merging behaviors
3. Incubating weak signals proactively

Gathering varied inputs and meticulously observing utilization patterns supplies raw material to detect early deviance. Leaders must also cultivate incubation to test anomalies, converting abstraction to actionable insights. Doing so transforms turbulence expectedly into a springboard for customized evolution.

The subsequent sections will examine practices firms employ scattering uncertainty by galvanizing nascent insights into purposeful experimentation. Anticipating transformations fortifies agility exceeding surface reactions alone.
Broadening sources instils perceptiveness by welcoming "strange" views challenging conventions. Netflix leverages user questionnaires identifying preferences before habits form, lately instructing moves into gaming.

Google likewise realized monetizing keyword data by speaking with advertising experts at a time when search was an infant industry. Unconventional questioning fuels innovative hypotheses.

Observing utilization patterns also yields clues through anomalies. YouTube detected short videos' popularity rise amongst young audiences before launching a mobile app and pioneering vertical content. Careful tracking subtle behaviors signals disruptive opportunities.

Leaders proactively incubate insights, guiding experimentation. Toyota connects R&D engineers directly with production crews capturing practical ideas previously deemed implausible. Cross-functional collaboration advances concepts from abstract to real world trials.

Anthropic cultivates safety research through "aligned assistant" project trials, rapidly learning without risking public consequences of failure compared to direct product development. Process strengthens resilience.

By systematically gathering varied inputs; diligently tracking emergent behaviors; and incubating weak signals through fast, low-risk prototyping, agile organizations respond proactively rather than reacting to disruptions. Anticipating change reshapes turbulence to advantage.

Leaders also form future-oriented taskforces gathering internal and external experts exploring potential areas. Netflix created an R&D lab investigating new domains before full-fledged entry like video games.

Anthropic convenes advisory boards including regulators and policymakers guiding research direction useful to diverse groups. Cross-pollination strengthens insight applicability.
Forward-scanning likewise monitors emerging professions for complementarity. 3M acquired bioinformatics startups leveraging newcomers' expertise long before competitors recognized implications.

Strategic scouting units systematically assess technologies addressing unsolved problems or satisfying latent needs. Autodesk acquires to fuel its vision of universal design accessibility through scanning promising innovators worldwide.

Intrapreneurship programs likewise seed ideas from within through "Shark Tank" style competitions. Anthropic awards seed funding, expert coaching and prototype resources for useful employee ideas. Internal incubation surfaces disruptors.

Strategic weak signal analysis, cross-pollinated futures taskforces and scouting latent technologies through acquisitions and Intrapreneurship programs enable anticipating shifts proactively rather than reactively responding to disruptions.
Agile leadership demands going beyond surface reactions by proactively identifying and cultivating weak signals years ahead of coming transformations. Broadening information sources through unconventional questioning and meticulously tracking emergent behaviors supplies raw insight into deviations indicative of opportunities.

Exemplar companies demonstrate systematizing generation and incubation of nascent concepts into actionable innovations. Forming future-focused taskforces and strategic monitoring emerging professions and technologies through scouting and acquisitions equips proactive experimentation exceeding status quo approaches.

Intrapreneurship programs additionally seed ideas from within by crowd-sourcing disruption potential from employee expertise. Together, these practices strengthen foresight capabilities beyond relying on disruptions finding organizations reactively.

Anticipating shifts position firms favorably meeting coming demands through customized evolution, rather than uncertainly responding to turbulence as it arrives. The next chapter section will discuss operating models cultivating an innovation-driven culture empowering agility through experimentation. This reinforces proactiveness as the new stability amid constant change.

2.3 Rethinking processes to increase flexibility

While scanning future landscapes and anticipating transformations strengthens agility, rigid internal structures can hinder adapting nimble execution. Bureaucratic processes optimized for stability undermine dexterity amid constant change. Leaders must scrutinize workflows for reinventing established patterns welcoming experimentation over blind adherence.

Toyota's famed production system epitomizes balancing efficiency with reinvention. Continuous improvement (kaizen) meant fluidly revising protocols as technologies evolved, avoiding entrenchment despite decades of dominance. Leaders cultivate analogous pliancy today by interrogating routines through lenses like:

1. Modularizing interdependence
2. Embracing failure as learning
3. Distributing control points

Fragmenting engrained interconnections; treating missteps transparently as lessons; and dispersing authority dismantles inertia. Doing so readies organizations fluidly orchestrating bespoke responses exceeding standardized playbooks.

The following examines practices realigned boosting operational dexterity. Streamlining bureaucratic overhead through such adjustments strengthens capacity for nimble pivots amid flux.

Modularizing mitigates fragility from interlaced dependencies. Automaker BMW structures factory subsystems independently enabling discrete units' shutdown without halting production. Agility results.

Anthropic decouples research areas into self-contained teams. While a cohesive direction guides new technologies, any team's struggles don't impede others. Resilience strengthens.

Embracing "intelligent failures" as lessons compels fluid reinvention. At Anthropic, research briefs transparently analyze theories disproven to spare duplication. Netflix too publishes stumbles aiding rivals. Learning outpaces protecting egos.

Strategic missteps also spur opportunities. Disney regained momentum by inviting Pixar's creative leadership after faltering with sequels. Humility enables agility surpassing initial limits.

Distributing control flattens response times. Zappos empowered frontline employees improving customer service amid the commerce revolution. Authority dispersed where impact manifests readies swift reactions.

Breaking concentration of power likewise multiplies innovation vectors. Cross-functional projects at Google spur ideas across divisions. Collaboration enfranchises diverse perspectives. Fluid resourcing also amplifies flexibility. Netflix reallocated 10% of its budget annually evaluating value. Funding follows opportunities rather than stabilizing past decisions.

Anthropic invites "flowability" by encouraging employees to self-direct between projects matching passions. Mobility counters silos with knowledge diffusion.

Reducing commitment to sunk costs through sunsetting outdated initiatives conserves capital for emerging areas. Alphabet disbanded lab divisions replacing strategies no longer fitting its vision. Resilience strengthens through reiterative portfolio evaluations.

Streamlining reports and removing unnecessary reviews trims inertia from decision cycles. At Netflix, leaders removed monthly reports focusing instead on annual objectives and frequent check-ins. Agility increases.

Embracing failing fast through rapid, low-cost experimentation also reduces risks from protracted initiatives. Anthropic iterates research directions weekly through minimal viable prototypes. Learning accelerates through frequent recalibration.

Together, these practices dismantle bureaucratic inertia by fragmenting interdependencies, treating failures transparently, distributing control points, and fluidly reallocating resources. Agility emerges from flexibility exceeding rigid processes.

Cross-functional budgeting further bolsters dexterity. Anthropic allocates venture-style funding across divisions stimulating ideas regardless of originating departments. Silos dissolve, collaboration flourishes.

Slashing unnecessary documentation through practices like auto-burial of outdated memos reduces friction impeding nimble decision-making. Zappos streamlines through sharing context digitally.

Colocation concentrates expertise to quicken coordination minus bureaucratic overhead. Pixar positioned animators near technologists fueling integral partnerships impossible through separate facilities.

Loosening preapprovals grants permissions where impact manifests. Anthropic offers informal research reviews, trusting teams' expertise. Judgement emancipates potential stalled awaiting hierarchy.

Reverse-mentoring younger staff also introduces fresh perspectives challenging conventions. Their queries surface ingrained habits ripe for reinvention. Reciprocity inspires multiplicative thought.

Rethinking processes dismantles inertia through practices fragmenting interdependencies, streamlining oversight, empowering judgement wherever impact emerges, and concentrating collaborative strengths. Agility materializes from embracing fluid reinvention exceeding rigid protocols. While scanning future landscapes and responding proactively to weak signals strengthens forward vision, leadership must also unshackle internal operations from rigid structures hindering nimble executions. Bureaucratic protocols optimized for past stability undermine dexterity demanded amid constant technological and social change.

Exemplar companies demonstrate re-examining workflows through diverse lenses dismantles engrained impediments to reinvention. Modularizing interdependencies, embracing failures transparently, distributing control and fluidly reallocating resources to emerging opportunities readies fluid reorchestration exceeding rigid playbooks.

Streamlining unnecessary documentation and oversight, cross-functionally sharing budgets, collocating expertise, and loosening preapprovals where impact emerges further emancipates potential stalled in hierarchies or sunken commitments.

Together, interrogating routines strengthens an innovation-driven culture beyond reliance on strategic planning alone. Organizational agility emerges through fluidly orchestrating bespoke reactions customized to transformations continually reconstructing competitive landscapes.

2.4 Managing transitions effectively

While cultivating foresight, flexibility and an innovation-driven culture arms agility, change must still be orchestrated prudently. Even reinvention demands judiciously stewarding transitions to minimize disruption. Leaders smooth flux by carefully attending human, operational and strategic dynamics throughout evolutionary phases.

Four interlocking lenses prove essential guiding transformations purposefully: communication, reskilling, aligning culture and establishing new metrics. Together, these empower customized responses smoothly adapting capabilities to reinvent advantage amid reconstituting landscapes. The following will examine managing transitional elements through:

1. Transparent communication
2. Reskilling and talent transitions
3. Aligning culture with emerging strategies
4. Adapting metrics for revised objectives

Judiciously attending human, structural and evaluation factors through these lenses readies seamless evolution exceeding disruption. Strategic yet empathetic change stewardship strengthens resilience exceeding surface-level reactions.

Transparent communication supplies context maintaining motivation amid ambiguity. At Anthropic, research updates and town halls frame challenges as collective, inspiring ownership of solutions.

Strategic brevity likewise focuses goals simply amid complexity. Netflix articulated its streaming pivot succinctly before details emerged, attracting vital early partners. Clarity steady's reinvention.

Reskilling and talent transition smooth capability evolution. Toyota empowered plant managers through intensive manufacturing curriculum minimizing production disruptions from newer models.
Anthropic offers skill-stretching rotations exposing employees to varied expertise, bolstering flexibility across teams. Fluid talent management readies change.

Aligning culture maintains momentum by reflecting emerging dynamics. As Blockbuster resisted digital disruption, it never embraced Netflix's risk-taking ethos fueling innovation necessary for survival. Vision must evolve.

Adapting metrics establishes new objectives avoiding sunk commitments. Netflix shifted from subscriber counts to viewing engagement, catalyzing original content investments without disrupting strategy mid-flight. Calibration enables nimble course-corrections.

Empathetic transitions also ease shifts by attentively handling impacts on personnel. Anthropic funds reskilling or career coaching for researchers displaced by strategic pivots.

Compassion minimizes disruption from fluid resourcing prevailing needs over people. At Toyota, voluntary transfers spare layoffs amid reorganizations for new priorities.

Strategic communication establishes a compelling future state energizing stakeholders. Netflix's vision of internet TV worldwide excited consumers ahead of content investments paying off. Clarity inspires commitment to change.
Gradual rollouts trial transformations at smaller scales before widespread implementation. Anthropic stages research overhauls incrementally versus abruptly shutting programs. Pause points assess readiness and refine approaches.
Culture pilots cultivate norms for emerging territories. Netflix established West Coast entertainment expertise through strategic acquisitions before national studio expansions. Prototyping reduces risks.

Strategic investment and divestment orchestrate capability evolution through portfolio reconstruction. Toyota divested declining divisions proactively to energize emerging nodes outpacing adaptation constraints. Change management integrates seamlessly.
External partnerships also facilitate transitions by mitigating disruption from internally driven changes. Toyota collaborated closely with suppliers throughout production shifts to distribute adjustments fluidly across ecosystems.

Anthropic enhances transparency cultivating external insight benefiting from technological progress without proprietary risks. Societal impacts guide research direction beyond organizational priorities alone.

Compelling career development makes shifts opportunities for growth versus disruption. Netflix positioned technical transitions as prospects for staff to broaden expertise critical to strategy. Meaning motivates change.

Distributing leadership stimulates shared commitment to reinvention that no single role could inspire. Netflix promoted Pilar Pagán from middle management to unprecedented content roles demonstrating fluid paths amid turbulence. Participation energizes.

Celebrating milestones maintains momentum through instability. Anthropic holds achievements—patents, publications and impact cases—for small wins empowering ongoing perseverance through challenges ahead. Appreciation steadies will.

Strategic yet empathetic transitions judiciously attend human, structural and evaluation dynamics throughout evolutionary phases. Together, these lenses smooth flux toward resilient yet purposeful evolution.

While cultivating foresight, flexibility and an innovation-driven culture arms agility, change must still be judiciously orchestrated to minimize disruption through transitional phases. Even amid strategic or technological reinvention, leaders must carefully steward human and operational dynamics.

Exemplar companies demonstrate navigating flux purposefully by transparently communicating evolving contexts, reskilling workforces, aligning culture with emerging strategies, and adapting metrics for revised objectives. Together, these lenses ease transitions exceeding surface-level reactions.

Empathetic practices like funding career coaching, gradually implementing changes, empowering small wins, and celebrating milestones also smooth disruption. External partnerships and compelling development opportunities further distribute impacts across wider ecosystems.

Strategic communication sustains momentum by envisioning compelling future states motivating commitment to change. Distribution of leadership likewise stimulates shared responsibility for reinvention.

Together, judiciously attending transitional elements through communication, talent management, cultural evolution and metric recalibration readies organizations smoothly adapting capabilities amid reconstituting environments. Resilience emerges from strategically yet empathetically orchestrating purposeful transformation.

Chapter 3
Fostering a Culture of Innovation

3.1 Encouraging creative problem solving

While cultivating agility through flexibility, proactive vision, and purposeful change depends upon navigating uncertain terrain, doing so demands creative approaches spanning established protocols. Leaders fuel resilience by inspiring innovation emancipated from rigid assumptions.

Four interlinked practices spark novel responses rising to reconstructing competitive dynamics: experimenting frequently yet prudently, diversifying perspectives in teams, reacting transparently to intelligent failures, and empowering judgment amid ambiguity. Together these strengthen potential exceeding expectations.

The following will examine encouraging creative problem solving through:

1. Embracing frequent, low-risk experimentation
2. Assembling diverse, cross-functional teams
3. Treating failures transparently as lessons
4. Loosening controls to empower frontline judgment

Judiciously combining these lenses ignites imagination navigating flux superseded by rote protocols. Adaptability emerges from innovation outstripping expectations amid reconstructing environments.

Embracing frequent, low-risk experimentation sparks novel solutions with minimal resource commitments. Anthropic rapidly prototypes research directions through weekly sprints.

Netflix popularized lean startup methodology, iteratively testing hypotheses at low budgets. Exploration outpaces assumptions while mitigating risks.

Assembling diverse, cross-functional teams stimulates ideas crossing specialized silos. Pixar combines technical and creative domains in unified story labs.

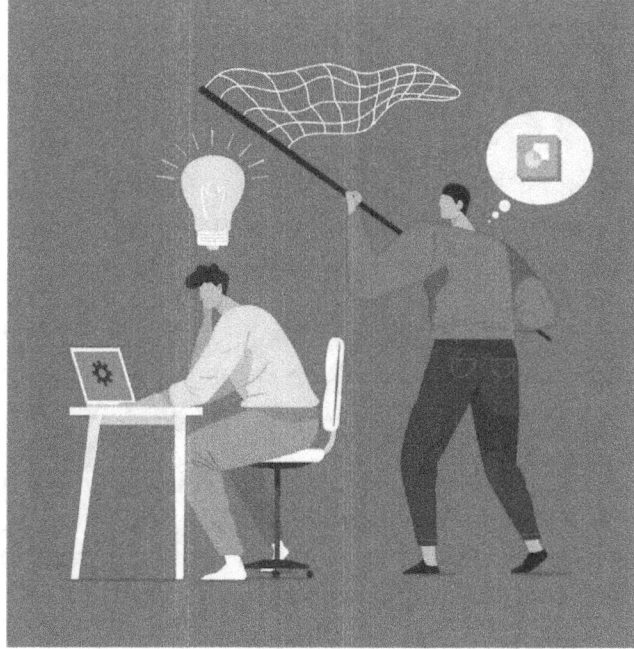

Multi-disciplinary researchers constantly exchange techniques across fields. Novel couplings germinate disruption-ready ideas. Treating failures transparently as lessons cultivates risk-taking by demystifying stumbles. Anthropic openly analyses theories disproven to inform ongoing inquiries.

Intelligent risks pave innovation exceeding safe trajectories when learnings diffuse organization-wide versus circumspectly internalizing struggles.

Loosening controls to empower frontline judgment ignites grassroots solutions amid complex challenges. Toyota tolerates annual failure quotas for production teams pursuing improvements.

Autonomy catalyzes bottom-up disruptors that centralized roadmaps could not envision. Judgement emancipates potentials awaiting directives.

Compensation also motivates calculated risk-taking beyond quarterly targets alone. Anthropic rewards scientific impact regardless publication timing to invent long-term pursuits.

Holistic career growth motivates frontlines innovating versus bureaucratic protocols alone. Netflix promoted data analysts into creative roles based on strategic vision beyond titles. Meaningful development inspires reinvention.

Strategic communication converts failures into exciting possibilities by reframing setbacks positively. When Anthropic's research faltered, leaders energized rebuilding through town halls spotlighting resilient perseverance. Adversity strengthens will

External insight further spark ideas from diverse perspectives. Anthropic cultivates outside researchers, partners and stakeholders to challenge mindsets fueling unexpected epiphanies. Societal impacts guide innovation beyond parochial pursuits.

Playful experimentation during work hours inspires organic creativity exceeding scheduled ideation. Toyota production teams tinker during breaks birthing industry-shaping kaizens. Joy breeds disruption.

Together, judiciously combining these lenses through frequent yet prudent experimentation, diverse collaborations exceeding silos, transparent failure treatments and frontline empowerment fuels imaginative reinvention exceeding rigid protocols.

Dedicated "skunkworks" also protect maverick projects from risk-averse bureaucracies. 3M created an incubator for post-it notes to follow curiosity wherever it led versus constrained deadlines. Sanctuary energizes innovation.

Hackathons concentrate diverse skills on unattached problems stimulating epiphanies beyond daily priorities. Anthropic's annual events birthed impactful ventures from researchers' earliest inclinations. Interruption spawns disruption.

Strategic retreats remove teams physically and mentally from routines energizing fresh perspectives on familiar challenges. Pixar's regular offsites dissolved assumptions fueling blockbuster stories. Distance inspires disruption.

Compelling internal ventures crowdfund grassroots ideas that resonate organization-wide versus reliance on directives alone. Anthropic researchers pitch proposals to colleagues who vote on favored pursuits with lab's discretionary budget. Passion fuels progress.

Together, these practices balance consistency with calculated risk-taking by protecting disruptors, concentrating skills temporarily on unattached problems, stimulating novelty through separation from routines, and energizing passions beyond priorities alone. Creativity thrives on the edge of chaos.

Where agility depends upon navigating uncertain terrain, leaders fuel resilience through inspiration exceeding expectations. Exemplar companies demonstrate judiciously combining practices encouraging calculated risk-taking like frequent yet prudent experimentation, diverse collaborations, transparent failure treatments, and frontline empowerment.

Together these spark novel solutions rising to reconstructing dynamics without depletion from inevitable stumbles. Compensation focusing on long-term impacts, holistic career growth, reframing setbacks positively, and external perspectives further motivate reinvention beyond protocols.

Dedicated disruptors, interruptive hackathons, strategic retreats removing teams physically and mentally from routines, and compelling grassroots ventures also concentrate imagination on unattached problems. Creativity emerges through inspiring innovation on the edge of chaos yet balanced with consistency.

Adaptability stems from imagination outstripping assumptions amid flux. Exemplars demonstrate judiciously combining lenses igniting novel responses exceeding expectations and emancipating potential from rigid mindsets alone. Together this strength resilience against uncertainty.

3.2　Supporting risk taking and experimentation

While creativity sparks disruption-ready ideas, trials cement potential through iterative refinements. Leaders cultivate experimentation by establishing psychologically safe environments separating intellectual risks from consequences.

Four interlinking practices foster calibrated testing: normalizing intelligent failures, linking compensation to impact not outputs, training risk literacy from early-career onboarding, and regularly evaluating learnings organization-wide. Together these embed iteration deeply.

The following will examine supporting risk taking and experimentation through:

1. Normalizing intelligent failure
2. Compensating for impact over outputs
3. Developing risk literacy from onboarding
4. Diffusing learnings organization-wide

Judiciously combining human, structural and cultural lenses through these practices institutionalizes calculated risk-taking beyond individual initiatives alone. Resilience matures through an experimentation-driven culture.

Normalizing intelligent failure cultivates risk-taking by establishing stumbles themselves pose no repercussions. Anthropic celebrates top errors openly as learning exemplars.

Mistakes detach from consequences inspiring further trials. Netflix's early shutdowns faced internally yet informed strategy pivots versus terminated careers. Safety motivates progress.

Compensating for impact over outputs rewards experimentation's intention exceeding superficial benchmarks. Anthropic weights grants for riskiness and scientific question versus publications alone.

Holistic impacts inspire multi-year pursuits beyond quarterly targets. Career paths likewise prioritize long-term impacts at Netflix over roles alone. Meaning sustains motivation.

Developing risk literacy from onboarding instils trial-and-error methodology from hiring. Anthropic researchers undergo risk workshops to normalize stumbles from project infancies.

Foundation strengthens willpower engaging uncertainty. Toyota production staff rotate roles absorbing failures naturally within continuous improvement culture. Habits institutionalize disruption.

Diffusing learnings organization-wide avoids siloed wisdoms by openly analyzing trials enterprise-wide. Anthropic town halls unpack failed theories benefiting all missions.

Transparency builds collective foresight exceeding any division. Resilience matures through shared understanding of uncertainty rather than its suppression.

Strategic communication also frames failures positively, when necessary, beyond factual reports. Anthropic reframed terminated projects as fulfilling their intention to inform future avenues versus personal shortcomings.

Reframing maintains momentum by energizing subsequent pursuits. Collaboration further sparks iterations when fluid exchanges outpace bureaucracy. Anthropic's interdisciplinary forums incubate ideas transcending silos.

Autonomy catalyzes exploration exceeding directives alone. Toyota spouses' grassroots improvements versus constraints from planners. Judgement scales disruption.

Playful competitions stimulate trials through incentives exceeding oversight. Netflix gamified data science competitions igniting brilliance beyond prescribed roles. Joy sparks progress.

Together, these lenses embed experimentation through establishing psychologically safe environments, judiciously incentivizing intention over outputs, cultivating risk literacy institutionally, allowing fluid collaboration and protecting calculated autonomy. Resilience matures through iterative refinement.

While creativity sparks disruptive ideas, trials cement potential through iterative refinement. Exemplar companies demonstrate cultivating an experimentation-driven culture by carefully combining key practices.

Normalizing failure as learning exempts risks from consequences, compensating for holistic impacts inspires long-term exploration beyond outputs, and developing risk literacy institutionally strengthens willpower engaging ambiguity. Transparently diffusing learnings enterprise-wide builds collective foresight exceeding any department as well.

Strategic reframing maintains momentum from stumbles, collaboration sparks fluid exchanges, empowered autonomy scales disruption, and playful competitions stimulate passions. Together these establish psychologically safe environments encouraging controlled variability.

Adaptability matures through an experimentation-driven culture where intelligent risks pose opportunities versus deterrents alone. Exemplars judiciously embed both innovation and iteration deep within operations. Resilience emerges from continuous refinement against reconstructing environments through calculated learning from mistakes.

3.3 Sustaining an experimentation mindset

While sparking creativity and embedding trial-and-error strengthen potentials, disruption-ready mindsets require constant fortification against rituals. Leaders nourish restless inquisitiveness through replenishing motivations, diversifying perspectives, and culturally instilling restlessness institutionally.

Four interlinking practices sustain curiosity exceeding status quos: recruiting disruptive talent prolifically, empowering sabbaticals renewing passions, benchmarking externally amid reconstructions, and playfully challenging core assumptions. Together these shields against complacency.

The following will examine sustaining an experimentation mindset through:

1. Recruiting disruptive talent extensively
2. Empowering sabbaticals for renewal
3. Benchmarking externally amid flux
4. Playfully challenging core assumptions

Judiciously combining human, structural and cultural lenses sustains disruptive mindsets institutionally. Resilience matures through restless inquisitiveness exceeding stability alone.
Recruiting disruptive talent extensively infuses organizations with instinctively inquisitive individuals. Anthropic targets recruit questioning status quos and publishing outside research networks.

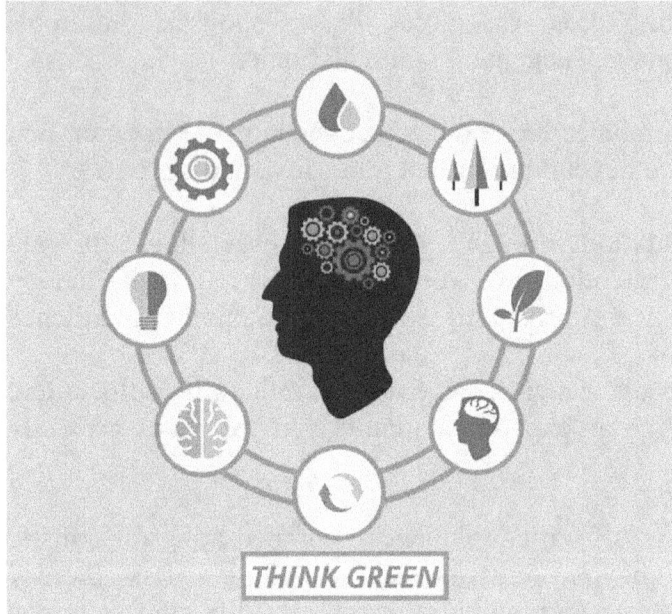

Fresh perspectives spark novel provocations. Netflix acquires technical experts from disconnected fields igniting ideas beyond homogenous pursuits. Diversity breeds disruption.

Empowering sabbaticals for renewal re-energize stagnating talents through exposure to disconnected innovators. Anthropic sponsors researchers transforming sectors through leaves amid academic communities.

Removal reinvigorates visionaries whose impacts matured past parochial mindsets. Renewed passion incarnates evolving missions.

Benchmarking externally amid flux prevents insular mindsets through studying reconstructions elsewhere. Anthropic regularly hosts outside thought leaders challenging directions.
Global purviews inspire disruption unbound from local successes. Exposure to variability strengthens flexibility.

Playfully challenging core assumptions provokes questioning rituals through debates minus reprisals. Anthropic workshops dismantle theories behind closed features to sharpen perspectives.

Safety inspires iconoclasm strengthening foundations. Unrest institutionalizes beyond individuals as culture evolves relentlessly.
Together, these practices replenish stagnating talents, diversify perspectives, and culturally instill restless curiosity.

Recruiting inquisitive individuals' counters institutional inertia. Sabbaticals recharge visionaries through immersion in disconnected communities. Benchmarking amid flux stimulates variability exceeding insularity.

Challenging assumptions playfully provokes iconoclasm where ideas prove impervious to scrutiny yet emerging stronger. Progress matures through reconstruction exceeding stability alone.

Strategic communication also frames failures as fuel for reconstruction versus critiques. Anthropic reframed terminated pursuits as serving the evolution of possibilities.

Reframing preserves willpower for subsequent disruption. Temporary failures find permanence through refinement versus termination.

Loose structures outpace rigid controls by incubating hypotheses fluidly. Anthropic's nimble forums cross-pollinate beyond silos' constraints.

Autonomy unleashes potentials where directives disperse grassroots strengths. Disruption thrives on judgement unfettered by protocols.

Together, these practices sustain inquisitiveness institutionally by replenishing stagnation, diversifying perspectives, inciting unrest culturally, and reframing tribulations constructively. Adaptability prevails through relentless evolution.

3.4 Recognizing and rewarding innovation

While sparking ideas, embedding trial-and-error, and sustaining restless curiosity, leaders must also diffuse disruptions organization-wide. Reward systems play a pivotal role by incentivizing reconstruction beyond local initiatives.

Four interlinking practices scale disruptions laterally: celebrating failures as precedents, granting compensation for impacts exceeding outputs, establishing innovation as a core competence, and crowdfunding grassroots visions company-wide. Together these incentivize adaptation institutionally.

The following will examine recognizing and rewarding innovation through:

1. Celebrating failures as precedents
2. Granting compensation for holistic impacts
3. Establishing innovation as a core competence
4. Crowdfunding grassroots visions company-wide

Judiciously combining human, structural and cultural lenses institutionally motivates calculated risk-taking and reconstruction enterprise-wide. Resilience strengthens through lateral diffusion of disruption.

Celebrating failures as precedents scales lessons by immortalizing stumbles as exemplars for subsequent trials.

Anthropic archives errors openly on internal forums inspiring others to iteratively build upon precedents fearlessly. Safety encourages many to learn from few.

Granting compensation for holistic impacts rewards disruptions' intentions exceeding outputs alone. Anthropic endows prizes for reconstructions' transformative potentials beyond publications.

Long-term visions outweigh short-term gains motivating perpetual betterment. Impacts scale with shared success.

Establishing innovation as a core competence elevates disruption to an institutional priority. Netflix positions artificial intelligence as its future beyond existing services.

Focus scales potentials when leaders diffuse restlessness cultural-wide. All staff accept reconstruction as duties rather than disruptors alone.

Crowdfunding grassroots visions company-wide incubates ideas laterally through democratic resourcing. Anthropic's forum allocates computing to proposals judged disruptive by peers.

Autonomy strengthens company-wide ownership of progress transcending top-down directives. Diffusion sparks when masses innovate collectively.
Together, these practices scale successes, motivate holistic impacts, establish restlessness institutionally, and empower collective reconstruction.
Celebrating failures preserves wills inspiring many through few's wisdom. Compensating visions outweighs outputs counteracting short-termism.

Establishing innovation as core shifts cultures enabling all staff reconstructing status quo. Crowdfunding grassroots visions strengthens ownership and collaboration beyond directives.

Strategic communication also frames disruption, scale and impact positively. Anthropic portrays terminated projects as serving wider potentials through disseminating learnings.

Reframing preserves reconstructive momentum. Transparency scales beneficence where isolated wisdoms fail to diffuse.

Loose structures exchange ideas fluidly bypassing silos' constraints. Anthropic forums collaborate borderlessly incubating visions.

Empowered judgement unleashes potentials exceeding governance protocols. Autonomy catalyzes grassroots strengths diffusing disruption organically.

Together, these practices incentivize and enable calculated risk-taking and reconstruction to permeate organizations laterally through exemplars, shared success, cultural priorities, and collective empowerment. Adaptation strengthens through enterprise-wide diffusion.
Playful competitions also stimulate grassroots inventions through time-bound challenges.

Netflix gamified data science tournaments crowdfunding brilliance beyond roles. Contests motivate disruptions from varied quarters converging on shared goals.

Loose affiliations outpace rigid hierarchies by enabling porous collaborations. Anthropic incubates ideas across silos through interdisciplinary forums.

Permeable structures seed innovations where top-down directives constrain emergent visions. Autonomy unleashes potentials beyond protocols.

Together, competitions, porous affiliations and autonomy inspire invention laterally by stimulating participation enterprise-wide, enabling cross-pollination beyond roles, and empowering judgements against rigid governance. Progress permeates institutions organically.

Chapter **4**

Building Resilience within Your Team

4.1 Cultivating psychological safety

While sparking disruptions, establishing adaptability institutionally ultimately relies on empowering individuals. Progress emerges through teams reconstructing possibilities together fearlessly.

Four linked attributes establish unconstrained inquisitiveness within groups: welcoming unfiltered ideas without repercussions, appreciating diverse perspectives equally irrespective of roles, establishing transparency amid uncertainties, and reframing jointly towards potentials exceeding limitations.

The following examines cultivating psychological safety through:

1. Welcoming unfiltered ideas without reprisals
2. Appreciating diverse perspectives equally
3. Establishing transparency amid ambiguities
4. Reframing jointly towards potentials

Together, these nurture unrestrained imagination collectively. Resilience arises through teams empowered to reinvent exceeding directives alone.

Welcoming unfiltered ideas without reprisals nurtures unrestrained imagination. Anthropic's forums encourage blue-sky thinking freed from realism's restraints.

Safety inspires visions unchecked by politics. Perspectives flourish where none face repercussions from dissent.

Appreciating diverse perspectives equally irrespective of roles strengthens flexibility. Netflix values engineers' visions alongside executives despite functions.

Equality cultivates unrest boundless to silos or pedigrees. Holistic views arise through interdisciplinary respect.

Establishing transparency amid uncertainties reinforces courage. Anthropic shares challenges and dead-ends with all to strengthen communal resilience.

Faith emerges through interdependence exceeding individual successes alone.

Strength matures through solidarity amid ambiguities.

Reframing jointly towards potentials counteracts limitations. Anthropic refashions terminated pursuits into building blocks for subsequent ideas.

Optimism inspires reconstruction exceeding any barrier. Progress arises through collectively pursued betterment versus isolated pursuits.
Together, these nurture unrestrained thinking, strengthen flexibility, reinforce courage through interdependence, and inspire optimism through collective reframing.

Welcome ideas freely exchanged uncensored self-expression. Appreciate diversity enabling holistic views. Transparency cultivates faith through communal effort.

Reframing jointly pursues potentials beyond any wall. Progress permeates where individuals support each other's visions exceeding any silo's constraints.

Playful techniques also energize teams beyond directives. Anthropic gamified collaborations like having researchers rate each other's ideas publicly.

Fun motivates participation and constructive critiques strengthening proposals boundlessly. Progress flourishes where work feels playful.

Loose affiliations foster innovation more organically than hierarchies. Anthropic enables fluid intersections transcending roles' limitations.

Permeability incubates visions beyond top-down mandates. Autonomy unleashes imagination exceeding governance alone.

Together, these nurture unrestrained creativity, energize participation, and incubate grassroots ideas through psychological safety, play, loose affiliations and collective autonomy. Teams reconstruct beyond directives collaboratively.
While sowing disruptions institutionally and diffusing reconstruction organizationally, leaders ultimately cultivate resilience by empowering teams psychologically.

Exemplar organizations demonstrate how welcoming unconstrained ideas fearlessly, appreciating diverse views equally, establishing transparency amid uncertainties, and reframing jointly towards potentials nurture unrestrained imagination collectively.

Playful techniques and loose affiliations further energize participation boundlessly. Together these practices establish psychological safety permeating groups and stimulating their communal capacity for reinventing beyond directives through interdependent support of each other's visions.

Progress emerges through teams reconstructing possibilities together fearlessly, drawing holistic perspectives from equals across divides, and reframing jointly towards betterment exceeding any barrier. Resilience arises intrinsically through groups empowered intrinsically to imagine beyond instructions alone.

4.2 Developing agility and resilience mindsets

While cultivating psychological safety liberates teams, leaders must also reinforce agility amid inevitable tribulations.

Four interconnected traits establish resilience mindsets amid disruptions: recognizing failures constructively exceeding criticism, reframing setbacks growth fully towards learnings, benchmarking variably amid dynamics, and sustaining adaptability culturally enduringly.

The following examines developing resilience mindsets through:

1. Recognizing failures constructively
2. Reframing setbacks growth fully
3. Benchmarking variably amid dynamics
4. Sustaining adaptability culturally

Together, these traits strengthen teams to persevere through reconstructing continually beyond directives alone. Progress matures through adaptive mindsets.

Recognizing failures constructively establishes precedents exceeding criticism.

Anthropic frames errors openly as building blocks to inspire subsequent incremental improvements. Learning motivates resilience exceeding blame.

Reframing setbacks growth fully towards learnings nourish determination.

Netflix repositions interruptions as opportunities to test assumptions and strengthen foundations for next reconstructions. Hope cultivates agility.

Benchmarking variably amid dynamics strengthens foundations. Anthropic compares trials diversely against multiple referents to extract versatile lessons beyond any fixity.

Flexibility matures through inter-contextual growth. Adaptability surpasses rigidity

Sustaining adaptability culturally endures reconstructing institutionally. Netflix reinforces company-wide reengineering continually against stasis.

Durability outweighs singular successes. Resilience perseveres through endemic traits withstanding disruptions institutionally over time.

Together, these traits cultivate reconstruction exceeding criticism, nourish hope through adaptable mindsets, and reinforce flexibility and perseverance institutionally through reframing and benchmarking resiliently. Teams strengthen change-readiness intrinsically.

Playful techniques also stimulate reconstructive mindsets lively.

Anthropic gamified ideation challenges researchers to iteratively remix and refine proposals against changing precedents. Fun motivates dynamism.

Loose structural affiliations cultivate variability more organically than rigid hierarchies. Permeable boundaries stimulate intersections across specialists fluidly.

Autonomy instils reconstructive orientations exceeding protocols' constraints. Intrinsic drive matures through self-directed growth beyond directives.

Together, play energizes participation and adaptation. Permeable structures stimulate cross-pollination. Autonomy cultivates self-determination and change-readiness endogenously.

Strategic communication also frames disruptions and flexibility positively. Netflix portrays renewed foundations as strengthening qualities resiliently against volatility.

Reframing pre-empts fears through hope. Transparency builds trust where mysteries constrained past pursuits.

Together, communication and framing cultivate reconstructive mindsets willingly as malleable strengths equipping teams enduringly. Motivation perseveres through communal narratives. While cultivating psychological safety liberates teams creatively, leaders complement flexibility by reinforcing resilience mindsets.

Exemplar organizations demonstrate how recognizing failures constructively, reframing setbacks growthfully, benchmarking variably and sustaining adaptability institutionally establish reconstructive orientations intrinsically.

Playful techniques, loose affiliations and autonomy further stimulate dynamism and self-directed change-readiness. Strategic communication frames disruptions and flexibility positively.

Together these practices cultivate reconstruction intrinsically exceeding any failure, nourish hope through inter-contextual growth, instil flexibility and perseverance through reframing and benchmarking adaptably.

Teams intrinsically mature change-ready, reconstructing continually beyond directives alone. Progress arises endogenously through communities empowered psychologically and equipped with resilient mindsets withstanding disruptions perseveringly through communal support.

4.3 Enhancing communication and collaboration

While cultivating psychological safety and resilience orientations, collaboration anchors teams enduringly through exchange.

Four interlinked attributes establish communication strengthening alliances constructively: actively soliciting diverse inputs proactively, appreciating contributions equally transparently, integrating insights synergistically, and celebrating progress communally.

The following examines enhancing collaboration through:

1. Actively soliciting diverse inputs proactively
2. Appreciating contributions equally transparently
3. Integrating insights synergistically
4. Celebrating progress communally

Together, these practices nourish participation and communal growth reinforce resilience relationally. Progress flourishes through interconnected endeavors
Actively soliciting diverse inputs proactively nurtures holistic exploration.
Anthropic design thinking workshops fostered equal participation encouraging all to propose perspectives beyond silos. Inclusion motivated interdisciplinary visions.
Appreciating contributions equally transparently reinforces value across divides.

Netflix showcases successes from varied divisions equally irrespective of functions or pedigrees to inspire participation organization-wide. Recognition motivates collaboration.

Integrating insights synergistically strengthens foundations communally.

Anthropic co-located multidisciplinary teams to test-run integrated solutions iteratively addressing nuances jointly beyond individual pursuits in isolation. Holism reinforced communal drive.

Celebrating progress communally nourishes communal spirit.

Netflix hosts monthly showcase parties recognizing plural contributions and team victories to inspire broader ownership and participation motivationally through a collaborative culture. Belonging anchored perseverance.
Playful techniques also foster collaboration lively.

Anthropic gamified ideation challenges teams to iteratively refine proposals coordinating interdependently. Fun motivated co-construction.

Loose yet accountable structures enhance spontaneity. Permeable boundaries stimulated intersections and spontaneity organically across specialists collaborating fluidly yet responsibly.

Together, play energized participation and collaboration while loose structures cultivated fluid intersections coordinating collaboratively yet accountably.

Strategic documentation and storytelling share tales cultivating future imaginings. Anthropic publishes project histories conveying lessons and catalyzing subsequent reconstructions communally.

Knowledge-sharing pre-empts silos and inspires holism. Transparency built interdependence where mysteries constrained communal drive in the past.

Celebratory and retrospective storytelling also reinforce progress through communal narratives. Reflecting on victories together nourishes perseverance and reconstructive spirit moving forward.

While cultivating psychological safety and resilience orientations, exemplar organizations demonstrate enhancing collaboration intrinsically through communal exchange.

Actively soliciting diverse inputs proactively, appreciating contributions transparently, integrating insights synergistically and celebrating progress communally nourish participation and communal spirit.

Playful techniques and loose accountable structures further foster fluid yet coordinated collaboration. Strategic documentation and storytelling cultivate future imaginings and strengthen interdependence.

Together these practices reinforce communal drive through inclusion, recognition, holism and belonging. Teams persevere through interconnected endeavors resolutely.

Progress arises endogenously where open exchange, playfulness and knowledge-sharing permeate relationships. Collaboration anchors resilience intrinsically as relationships strengthen mutually through sharing successes and lessons relationally towards collective betterment.

4.4 Establishing fail-fast feedback loops

While cultivating psychological safety, resilience and collaboration, agile feedback fortifies reconstruction iteratively.

Four interdependent traits reinforce fail-fast feedback loops strengthening foundations: establishing experimentation as preferred problem-solving, benchmarking assumptions persistently, iterating solutions cooperatively, and reassessing directives adaptively.

The following examines establishing fail-fast feedback loops through:

1. Establishing experimentation as preferred problem-solving
2. Benchmarking assumptions persistently
3. Iterating solutions cooperatively
4. Reassessing directives adaptively

Together, these practices nourish persistent reconstruction optimally aligned with realities dynamically. Progress matures through iterative realignment.

Establishing experimentation as preferred problem-solving cultivates rapid prototyping.

Anthropic researchers pursue minimum viable product experimentation to test possibilities nimbly before substantial investment. Iterative testing optimized solutions.

Benchmarking assumptions persistently against realities anchors visions objectively.

Netflix A/B tests suspect assumptions quantitatively against user behaviors relentlessly to discern impact factually before unwarranted scaling. Objectivity fortified strategies.

Iterating solutions cooperatively broadens perspectives constructively.

Anthropic collocated product teams jointly reconstructed solutions in design sprints incorporating multifaceted stakeholder inputs to strengthen nuanced improvements collaboratively. Inclusion optimized reconstructions.

Reassessing directives adaptively instils dynamic alignment.

Netflix revisited quarterly objectives qualitatively against market unexpected proactively recalibrating nimbly towards emerging imperatives. Agility surmounted volatility.

Playful prototyping also stimulates iterative experimentation creatively.

Anthropic research teams rapidly 3D printed whimsical prototypes to explore fringe possibilities entertainingly before committing substantial resources towards confirmed potentials. Fun stimulated exploration.

Structures balance stability with dynamism judiciously. Anthropic applies adaptive governance flexibly aligning accountabilities gradually against evolving exigencies. Judiciousness accommodated flux.

Autonomy complements top-down directives judiciously. Researchers' self-direct iterative reconstructions complementing institutional recalibrations for optimal symbiosis. Coordination optimized agility.

Together playful experimentation, adaptive structures and balanced autonomy-direction stimulated reconstruction cooperatively ensuring continual symbiotic realignment.

Documentation and showcase also cultivate iterative accountability and learning openly. Anthropic publishes experimental methodologies and reconstructions transparently cultivating future advancements communally.

Knowledge-sharing established interdependence towards perpetual progress where mysteries constrained drive in the past. Revelation fortified communal reconstruction.

Chapter **5**
Leading with Empathy and Connection

5.1 Understanding different perspectives

While building resilience within, exemplar leaders also cultivate fortitude beyond through empathetic connection across boundaries.

Four interdependent attributes establish understanding different perspectives constructively: listening actively for nuances non-judgmentally, reflecting perspectives back empathetically, finding common ground cooperatively, and acknowledging contexts appreciatively.

The following examines understanding different perspectives through:

1. Listening actively for nuances non-judgmentally
2. Reflecting perspectives back empathetically
3. Finding common ground cooperatively
4. Acknowledging contexts appreciatively

Together, these practices nourish collaborative will and fortify social robustness proactively beyond directives alone. Progress matures relationally across divides.

Listening actively for nuances non-judgmentally cultivates understanding across differences. As the leader of Anthropic, Dario Amodei places full attention on each speaker, making eye contact and asking gentle clarifying questions to ensure all aspects of perspectives are heard without assessment. This opens communication and allows for viewpoints to be shared openly.

Reflecting perspectives back empathetically validates each vantage point. As CEO of Netflix, Reed Hastings repeats back what he hears from employees and stakeholders to affirm their realities before providing any feedback of his own. This demonstrates comprehension and respect for different experiences. It also prevents premature solutions, instead focusing on true understanding.

Finding common ground cooperatively in initial disagreements builds bridges across borders. As facilitator of discussions, Amodei looks for shared values or objectives that can unite differing parties at the outset of debates. Even small areas of accord help interdependent progress and prevent entrenchment, allowing eventual synthesis of perspectives instead of an embroiled fragmentation.

Acknowledging contexts appreciatively recognizes the formative conditions behind opposing stances. Hastings ensures team discussions and leadership communications reference the situational challenges or uncertainties that potentially inform alternative stands. Validating contexts behind viewpoints prevents oversimplified othering and makes diverse stances more intelligible and inclusive to address constructively together.

Together, active listening without judgment, empathetic perspective reflecting, cooperative common ground seeking and appreciative context acknowledging nurture understanding across divisions. Leaders avoid premature solutions to first grasp stakeholder realities fully in their own terms.

Follow-up questioning and reiteration ensures clarity and checks assumptions. Amodei and Hastings regularly restate what they've heard to confirm comprehension, and pose gentle questions to remove any ambiguities in perspectives shared. This validity establishes trust in the exchange.

Storytelling also renders situational experience more palpable. Harboring specific examples makes abstract perspectives tangible and helps shift mental models. Leaders sharing formative experiences of their own cultivates relatability and diffuse defensiveness.

Empathetic enquiry reinforces inclusion where division may persist otherwise. It nurtures collaborative will emerging from within stakeholder realities recognized, rather than externally imposed visions. Stakeholders feel heard and motivated to co-construct given ownership over the exchange.

Progress arises endogenously as connections form across disconnects and joint interests emerge from currently disparate stands explored not in opposition but from within each other. Documentation and communal reflection further embed understanding institutionally.

Anthropic publishes leadership discussion summaries to cultivate iterative comprehension organizationally. Iterative grasping of nuanced views becomes embedded rather than solitary or transient.

Retrospective storytelling also strengthens capacity for perspective. Netflix leadership conferences review how viewpoints evolved relationally through deep discussion. This reinforces capacity for empathetic exchange as an organizational competency.

Communities that comprehend differences intrinsically become change-ready organically. Realities coordinately recognized cultivate communal reconstruction desire from within.

5.2 Engaging people with compassion

While cultivating understanding across differences, compassionate engagement also fortifies communal support proactively.

Four interdependent qualities establish compassionate engagement: demonstrating care authentically through deep interest, empowering autonomy through ownership encouragement, celebrating progress communally through recognition, and reconstructing cooperatively through inclusive problem-solving.

The following examines compassionate engagement through:

1. Demonstrating care authentically through deep interest
2. Empowering autonomy through ownership encouragement
3. Celebrating progress communally through recognition

4. Reconstructing cooperatively through inclusive problem-solving

Together, these practices nurture fortitude emerging endogenously as stakeholders support one another amid disruptions. Community matures relationally.

Demonstrating care authentically through deep interest builds goodwill. As Anthropic's CEO, Amodei rotates tasks to understand contextual realities first-hand and genuinely inquires about wellbeing frequently. This cultivates intrinsic motivation over directive compliance through tangible concern.

Empowering autonomy through ownership encouragement instils stakeholder fortitude. Netflix founder Hastings delineates loose structures with adaptive governance, allowing teams self-directed reconstruction. This nourishes intrinsic drive and stakeholder-led change-readiness organically in fluctuating conditions.

Celebrating progress communally through recognition shares victories relationally. At quarterly summits, Anthropic highlights personal breakthrough stories of researchers publicly. Recognition kindles interdependent spirit over competition and attracts interest in the organization's purpose.

Reconstructing cooperatively through inclusive problem-solving cultivates collaborative will. Hastings invites multi-level stakeholder input in strategic reassessment to bring diverse strengths when confronting challenges. Incorporating various standpoints stimulates reconstruction emerging endogenously.

Together, authentic care demonstration, ownership encouragement, communal progress celebration and inclusive reconstruction nourish fortitude emerging endogenously as stakeholders uphold one another amid disruptions.

Interest driven dialogue during rotations at Anthropic strengthens understanding across functions for coordination during crises. Shared burdens cultivate interconnected support networks organically.

Loose governance and adaptive structures at Netflix mature autonomy while ensuring flexible direction during volatility. Self-organized teams reconstruct rapidly utilizing diverse expertise.

Public victory narratives published by Anthropic kindles perseverance as challenges surface through relating progress motivationally. Communal spirit sustains efforts collectively.

Reconstructions informed by multi-level input at Netflix brings holistic realism optimizing solutions for complex problems. Diverse expertise feels incorporated towards navigating disruptions coordinately.

Documentation and reflection further embed this capacity for compassionate fortification institutionally. Anthropic periodically reviews success stories qualitatively to track emergent themes in communal care, ownership and reconstructions strengthens. Institutionalizing compassion develops organizational crisis-resiliency.

5.3 Inspiring purpose and commitment

While cultivating understanding and compassionately engaging people, exemplar leaders also guide purpose and commitment intrinsically.

Four interdependent practices establish purpose and commitment inspiration: envisioning significance authentically, communicating impacts motivationally, demonstrating milestones regularly, and sustaining progress cooperatively.

The following examines inspiring purpose and commitment through:

1. Envisioning significance authentically
2. Communicating impacts motivationally
3. Demonstrating milestones regularly
4. Sustaining progress cooperatively

Together, these practices nurture fortitude emerging endogenously as purpose unites diverse efforts amid disruptions. Commitment matures intrinsically.

Envisioning significance authentically instills true north. As Anthropic's founder, Dario Amodei articulates how human-based AI can augment scientific discovery to benefit humanity, establishing a compelling higher purpose beyond directives.

Communicating impacts motivationally spreads unified vision. Netflix CEO Reed Hastings publishes qualitative impact reports highlighting how streaming media expands access to culture and stories worldwide. This inspires intrinsic identification with purpose across levels.

Demonstrating milestones regularly embeds purpose accountably. Anthropic celebrates technological achievements and scientific breakthroughs routinely to tangible progress toward significance. Reaching targets intrinsically fuels further efforts.

Sustaining progress cooperatively nourishes commitment endogenously. Hastings incorporates quarterly strategy reviews inviting all levels to coordinate efforts and reconstruct approaches communally. Grassroots commitment to a shared higher purpose emerges intrinsically over directives.

Together, authentic envisioning, motivational sharing, regular demonstrating and cooperative sustaining of progress guide purpose emerging endogenously as significance unites diverse efforts amid disruptions.

Articulation of significance at Anthropic develops long-term intrinsic alignment over short-term metrics. Employees internalize a compelling why beyond directives.

Impact reports at Netflix spread contagious identification with how streaming expands access to stories globally. Employees intrinsically align efforts toward a shared higher purpose.

Consistent celebrating of technical breakthroughs at Anthropic nourishes accountability to evolve science for humanity's benefit. Progress accountability fuels further intrinsic motivation.

Quarterly reviews inviting grassroots input at Netflix sustain commitment as purpose reconstructs cooperatively. Employees feel ownership over navigating disruptions coordinated by a higher purpose.

Together, envisioning a compelling why, sharing impacts motivationally, demonstrating accountability to purpose through progress, and cooperatively reconstructing approaches nurture fortitude emerging endogenously as stakeholders commit to a shared higher significance. Documentation of narratives, milestones and strategy reflections archive purposes evolving organically. Communities intrinsically perpetuate vision amid flux.

5.4 Facilitating team cohesion during change

While cultivating understanding, engaging compassionately and inspiring purpose, exemplar leaders also facilitate team cohesion amid change intrinsically.

Four interdependent qualities establish team cohesion during change: cultivating psychological safety through vulnerability, promoting plurality through diversity, integrating roles collaboratively, and advancing communally through celebrations.

The following examines facilitating team cohesion through:

1. Cultivating psychological safety through vulnerability
2. Promoting plurality through diversity
3. Integrating roles collaboratively
4. Advancing communally through celebrations

Together, these practices nurture fortitude emerging endogenously as teams reconstruct change cooperatively. Cohesion matures relationally.

Cultivating psychological safety through vulnerability builds trust. Netflix CEO Reed Hastings openly discusses failure learning to promote risk-taking without blame. This establishes compassion amid disruptions for grassroots ideas catalyzing reconstructive innovation.

Promoting plurality through diversity fosters holism. Anthropic leadership ensures gender, ethnic and disciplinary representation across functions and levels. Heterogeneity advances reconstructive solutions capitalizing on varied viewpoints intrinsically.

Integrating roles collaboratively stimulates ownership. Hastings invites cross-level training exchanges rotating staff between technical and strategic positions. Mutual understanding between expertise naturally facilitates coordinated reconstructing.

Advancing communally through celebrations shares victories relationally. Quarterly summits publicize team progression stories to prompt communal spirit over competition. Intrinsic fortitude emerges empowered through interdependence amid disruptions.

Together, vulnerability, diversity, collaborative role integration and communal celebrations nurture fortitude emerging endogenously as teams reconstruct change cooperatively through cohesion.

Open failure discussions at Netflix cultivate safety for innovation from grassroots. Compassion emerges intrinsically amid disruptions.

Heterogeneous representation at Anthropic stimulates reconstruction capitalizing on varied perspectives organically. Teams advance holistically.

Cross-training exchanges at Netflix naturally facilitate coordination between expertise for flexibility. Mutual understanding optimizes reconstruction.

Quarterly story sharing at Anthropic prompts communal spirit sustaining efforts relationally. Intrinsic fortitude emerges empowered through interdependence amid turbulence.

Together, vulnerability, diversity, integration and celebrations reinforce fortitude as teams reconstruct change cooperatively. Trust, plurality, ownership and interdependence cultivate cohesion maturing relations amid disruptions.

Recording reflections and interactions archives cohesion factors developing organically. Leaders rebuild by recognizing realities to nurture community's emergent strengths. Documentation preserves capacities for future adaptability.

Chapter **6**

Visioning with Scenarios and Strategic Options

6.1 Thinking systemically about the future context

Exemplar leaders envision reconstructing amid uncertainty systematically through context scenarios.

Four practices establish systemic contextualization: mapping trends expansively, exploring causality profoundly, considering perspectives pluralistically, projecting alternatives imaginatively.

The following examines thinking systemically about future context through:

1. Mapping trends expansively
2. Exploring causality profoundly
3. Considering perspectives pluralistically
4. Projecting alternatives imaginatively

Together, these nurture adaptability as communities reconstruct contextually amid disruptions. Systemic foresight cultivates strategic flexibility.

Mapping trends expansively establishes interconnections. Anthropic leadership connects AI development with societal, economic and policy influences to understand reconstruction opportunities holistically.

Exploring causality profoundly acknowledges interdependencies. Netflix examines how streaming expansion enables remote work and socialization, considering indirect consequences of strategic decisions.

Considering perspectives pluralistically fosters co-creation. Anthropic hosts cross-sector discussions embracing diverse viewpoints on humanity-centered AI's impacts to develop context scenarios collectively.

Projecting alternatives imaginatively stimulates adaptability. Netflix envisions how pandemic-induced isolation could accelerate blended virtual/live experiences and how this shapes future technological and cultural directions differently.

Together, expansive mapping, profound causality exploration, pluralistic perspective incorporating and imaginative projecting reinforce systemic contextual awareness as communities strategize reconstruction contextually.

Connecting AI to wider influences at Anthropic establishes systemic understanding of reconstruction opportunities.

Examining streaming's broader impacts at Netflix acknowledges consequences of strategic choices.

Cross-sector perspective co-development at Anthropic fosters co-creation of context scenarios. Imaginative pandemic alternatives at Netflix stimulate adaptability through different cultural and technological pathways.

Together these cultivate systemic foresight for contextual reconstruction. Documentation archives interconnecting landscapes and implications maturing communities' strategic flexibility.

Leaders appreciate realities to nurture communities' emergent capacities through mapping expansively, exploring causality profoundly, considering pluralism and projecting imaginatively. Developing context awareness endogenously optimizes navigating disruptions cooperatively.

Recording discussions preserves systemic thought developing organically. Communities gain foresight to proactively coevolve strategies and context intrinsically aligned. Exemplars guide change recognizing realities to seed reconstructive adaptation from within.

6.2 Crafting multiple vision and strategy options

Visioning flexibility demands crafting multiple strategic alternatives. Four practices establish optionality: brainstorming divergently, envisioning credibly, balancing desirability and feasibility comprehensively, prioritizing pragmatically.

The following examines crafting vision and strategy options through:
1. Brainstorming divergently
2. Envisioning credibly
3. Balancing desirability and feasibility comprehensively
4. Prioritizing pragmatically

Together, these cultivate reconstructive adaptability amid disruption. Communities gain optionality intrinsically motivating exploration of pathways situated strategically.

Brainstorming divergently stimulates novelty. Netflix invites grassroots input to envision how decentralized media production and distribution could leverage user-tailored experiences differently.

Envisioning credibly establishes plausibility. Anthropic constructs detailed narratives of decentralizing AI development under alternative compliance and investment scenarios globally to variably impact humanity.

MARKETING STRATEGY

Balancing desirability and feasibility comprehensively considers adaptability. Netflix weighs aspirations like hyper-personalization against realities including infrastructure dependencies to establish reconstructive roadmaps.

Prioritizing pragmatically phases exploration. Anthropic sequences concept proving, scaled piloting and socialization before full transitions to optimize learning through disruptive changes incrementally.

Together, divergent thinking, credible envisioning, balanced assessment and pragmatic prioritization cultivate optionality for reconstructing situatively amid uncertainty.

Grassroots input at Netflix stimulates novel perspectives on decentralized media experiences.

Detailed narratives at Anthropic establish alternative compliance and investment scenarios' plausibility globally.

Weighing aspirations against realities at Netflix establishes reconstructive roadmaps considerately.

Incremental pacing at Anthropic optimizes disruption navigation and learning collectively.

Together these cultivate situative flexibility for communities navigating uncertainty. Documentation of options matures strategic nimbleness amid change.

Leaders appreciate stakeholder realities to seed explorative capacities endogenously. Recording visioning enriches collective foresight navigating innovatively.

Communities gain optionality through divergent thinking, credible envisioning, balanced assessments and pragmatic prioritization cultivated cooperatively. Strategic nimbleness emerges intrinsically for contextual reconstruction.

Exemplars guide change by nurturing communities' emergent visioning muscles situatively in service of humanity. Multiple pathways seed reconstructive adaptability navigated cooperatively.

Exemplar leaders cultivate optionality through brainstorming divergently, envisioning credibly, balancing desirability and feasibility comprehensively, and prioritizing pragmatically.

Grassroots input at Netflix stimulates novel perspectives on decentralized experiences. Detailed scenarios at Anthropic establish plausibility of systemic impacts.

Weighing aspirations and realities at Netflix establishes considerate roadmaps. Incremental pacing at Anthropic optimizes disruption navigation collectively.

Together these practices nourish situative flexibility for communities navigating unpredictably. Documentation matures strategic agility amid turbulence.

Leaders appreciate stakeholder viewpoints to develop explorative capacities endogenously. Recording visioning enrichers cooperative foresight.

Communities gain optionality through cultivating divergent thinking, credible envisioning, balanced assessments and pragmatic prioritization. Strategic nimbleness emerges intrinsically for contextual reconstruction.

Exemplars guide change by nurturing communities' emergent visioning abilities situatively. Multiple pathways need reconstructive adaptability navigated cooperatively and contextually.

6.3 Mapping weak signals and black swans

Amid uncertainty, weak signals foreshadow disruption while black swans represent unpredictability. Exemplar leaders orient around these phenomena through mapping patterns proactively.

Four practices establish such mapping: tracking extensively, connecting creatively, questioning inquisitively, learning adaptively.
The following examines mapping weak signals and black swans through:

1. Tracking extensively
2. Connecting creatively
3. Questioning inquisitively
4. Learning adaptively

Together, these seed adaptabilities for reconstructing amid turbulence intrinsically navigated cooperatively.
Tracking extensively establishes pattern noticing. Netflix aggregates streaming expansions alongside user location/activity data to identify demographic shifts enabling remote productions.

Connecting creatively unveils insights. Anthropic links AI streamlining with industrial automation increase to question job transformations' wider societal impacts.

Questioning inquisitively stimulates novelty. Netflix explores how blended virtual/live experiences could reshape education through polling unconventional perspectives.

Learning adaptively incorporates reconnaissance. Anthropic archives intersectional issues surfaced to reconsider contextual priorities and socialization methods iteratively.

Together, extensive tracking, creative connecting, inquisitive questioning and adaptive learning fortify weak signal identification and black swan preparedness amid uncertainty. Communities gain resilience.
Aggregating data at Netflix identifies patterns enabling remote productions.
Linking trends creatively at Anthropic questions job transformations' societal impacts.
Exploring blended experiences' education impacts at Netflix through diverse polling.

Archiving intersectional issues at Anthropic to reconsider priorities and socialization.

Together these practices strengthen weak signal discernment and black swan readiness amid unpredictability. Documentation cultivates community resilience.

Leaders appreciate realities to endogenously develop weak signal and black swan discovery muscles. Recording mappings nourishes collective foresight.

Communities gain resilience through cultivating extensive tracking, creative connecting, inquisitive questioning and adaptive learning cooperatively. Reconnaissance empowers reconstructive adaptability.

Exemplars guide change by nurturing communities' emergent mapping abilities situatedly. Multiple pathways seed disruption navigation navigated contextually.

6.4 Aligning around strategic imperatives

Grounding in strategic imperatives aligns communities amid recalibration. Four practices establish directionality: articulating priorities clearly, focusing purposefully, mobilizing cooperatively, iterating responsively.

The following examines aligning around strategic imperatives through:
1. Articulating priorities clearly
2. Focusing purposefully
3. Mobilizing cooperatively
4. Iterating responsively

Together, these seed reconstructive momentum navigating disruption cooperatively and agilely amid change.

Articulating priorities clearly at Netflix centered user-tailoring amid platform shifts. Focusing purposefully at Anthropic on beneficence guided AI augmentation responsibly.

Mobilizing cooperatively across sectors at Anthropic aligned partner networks towards inclusion pragmatically.

Iterating responsively at Netflix to pandemic impacts accelerated personalized experiences appropriately.

Together, clear prioritization, focused mobilization, cooperative alignment and responsive recalibration have established directionality adaptively amid disruption.

Centering on user tailoring at Netflix clarified strategic direction amid transition.

Steering by beneficence at Anthropic focused efforts guiding AI development responsibly.

Cooperatively aligning networks at Anthropic united partners pursuing inclusion pragmatically. Recalibrating nimbly to impacts at Netflix accelerated personalized experiences appropriately.

Together these practices grounded communities in priorities, concentrating efforts, cooperation and agility amid disruption. Documentation fortified momentum.

Leaders appreciate stakeholder viewpoints, nourishing intrinsic directionality development. Recording imperatives bolsters collective navigational mastery.

Communities gain momentum through cultivating clear prioritization, focused cooperation, joint alignment and responsive recalibration. Reconstruction strengthens intrinsically.

Exemplars guide change by nurturing communities' emergent alignment abilities situatively. Multiple pathways seed agile disruption steering contextually.

Chapter **7**

Agile Strategy Development and Execution

7.1 Planning iteratively using sprints and milestones

Agile strategy development embraces nonlinear collaboration through iterative sprints and milestones. Four practices enable such nonlinearity: rapid prototyping, testing incrementally, integrating adaptively and reflecting collectively.

The following examines planning iteratively using sprints and milestones through:

1. Rapid prototyping
2. Testing incrementally
3. Integrating adaptively
4. Reflecting collectively

Together, these cultivate agile recalibration amid uncertainty navigated cooperatively.

Rapid prototyping at Netflix yielded accelerated testing of interface variations surfacing usability insights.

Incremental testing at Anthropic of modified algorithms unveiled societal impact tradeoffs pragmatically.

Adaptive integrating across sectors at Netflix synchronized localized expansions seamlessly amid transitions.

Collective reflecting at Anthropic on developmental impacts reinforced beneficence prioritization adaptively.

Together, sprint-focused prototyping, incremental experimentation, cross-team integration and reflection have enabled agile recalibration amid transition.

Netflix employed rapid prototyping techniques to quickly test interface variations and evaluate usability. New ideas were brought to life through paper prototypes, digital mockups, or basic code. This allowed different design options to be tested immediately with real users providing feedback. Incremental improvements could then be made and retested through multiple short sprint cycles. Over time, this process surfaced valuable insights around things like navigation flows or playback controls that ultimately led to a more seamless user experience.

Anthropic took an incremental testing approach to modifying their algorithms. Small, targeted changes would be made and the outputs carefully analyzed to identify any unintended societal or fairness impacts. By starting small and evaluating after each step, they could build understanding around complex issues like bias or accessibility. Problems could be addressed without wholesale changes, preserving stability while still advancing the model. This pragmatic method reinforced their commitment to developing AI that is robust and beneficial.

At Netflix, adaptive integration across international engineering teams helped synchronize localized expansions seamlessly amid continuous transitions in the business. Through integration sprint planning and tracking progress iteratively, teams could rapidly share new features, designs or infrastructure changes. This enabled a unified product vision and customer experience even as Netflix grew into new regions and markets.

Collective reflecting at Anthropic's weekly all-hands meetings on developmental and partnership activities reinforced their prioritization of beneficence. Opportunities to re-examine impacts and priorities informed planning for subsequent sprints to reinforce their commitment to creating technology that helps, not harms, humanity.

7.2 Establishing key performance indicators

Establishing clear yet adaptable metrics guides iterative refinement. Four practices reinforce indicativity: setting contextual targets, measuring holistically, comparing meaningfully, adjusting responsively.
The following examines establishing key performance indicators through:

1. Setting contextual targets
2. Measuring holistically
3. Comparing meaningfully
4. Adjusting responsively

Together, these cultivate quantitative and qualitative oversight enabling agile recalibration amid transition navigated cooperatively.
Netflix set viewing targets contextualized to local markets, considering internet speeds and cultural preferences ensuring representative guidance.

Anthropic measured holistically against metrics like fairness, privacy and safety buoying responsible advancement amid variability and turbulence.
Meaningfully comparing KPIs quarterly across sectors highlighted adjustment opportunities, safeguarding continued progress cooperatively.
Responsively adjusting indicators emphasized agility, aligning metrics to emerging priorities like accessibility proactively amid disruption.

Together, contextualizing goals, encompassing measurement, purposeful benchmarking and receptive refining have established oversight amid dynamical change.
At Netflix, setting contextualized viewing targets involved careful analysis of each local market. Factors like average internet speeds, device preferences, content availability and cultural viewing norms were considered. Rather than rigid one-size-fits-all goals, targets

acknowledged the realities of each region. This ensured the targets provided actually representative and useful guidance that could flexibly accelerate or uphold progress as needed. It also gave local teams agency to best optimize for success within their unique environment.

Anthropic measured their progress holistically against indicators beyond just financial metrics. They tracked factors such as algorithmic fairness, privacy preservation, potential for misuse and overall safety. This more well-rounded approach helped buoy continued advancement even as individual KPIs varied, reflecting the complex nature of their work. It also reinforced their commitment to developing technology responsibly and for the benefit of humanity.

On a quarterly basis, Anthropic and Netflix would meaningfully compare KPIs within and across high-level functions and divisions. This process highlighted opportunities for adjustment by surfacing differences, correlations or deviations from expectations in their metrics. It initiated thoughtful review of what was working well or where more effort may be needed. This collaborative benchmarking aided in continuously improving their strategies cooperatively over time.

Adjusting indicators in a responsive manner allowed Anthropic to emphasize agility. As priorities shifted towards areas like accessibility, metrics were re-centered to best reflect and guide progress. This proactive recalibration kept oversight closely aligned to emerging strategic imperatives and challenges amid dynamic industry changes.

7.3 Fostering a test-and-learn approach

Fostering a test-and-learn ethos cultivates proficiency amid uncertainty. Four practices reinforce such an ethos: conducting many lightweight experiments, failing productively, distributing learnings transparently, institutionalizing reflexively.
The following examines fostering a test-and-learn approach through:

1. Conducting many lightweight experiments
2. Failing productively
3. Distributing learnings transparently
4. Institutionalizing reflexively

Together, these practices seed reconstructive momentum navigating disruption cooperatively and iteratively.
At Netflix, conducting many lightweight experiments allowed ideas to be validated quickly through small, low-risk tests. New features or minor product changes could be tried out on a limited sample of users. This generated feedback to assess whether broader implementation

was warranted. It also minimized potential downsides from failures. This rapid experimentation on the margins helped accelerate optimization of the core experience.

When experiments at Netflix failed to achieve desired outcomes, the teams focused on failing productively. Rather than seeing it as a setback, negative results provided valuable learning. Outcomes were analyzed to understand why users responded the way they did. Armed with these insights, adjustments could be made and new hypotheses explored. Over time, this cultivated a culture where risks were embraced for the knowledge gained, not avoided for potential embarrassment.

Anthropic took an open approach to distributing learnings transparently across departments and with partner organizations. After each sprint and project, they would conduct retrospective sessions to capture and share what was learned, including details on failures or challenges faced. This prevented duplicated efforts and encouraged continuous improvement as knowledge was built upon communally. It also strengthened collaborative muscles throughout their network.

Institutionalizing reflexive reviews at Anthropic helped seed a test-and-learn foundation that could weather disruption and personnel changes. Streamlining the sharing of experiences into repeatable processes ensured each new member could readily access historical knowledge. It also formalized a structure for strategizing iteratively as contexts evolved over time.

Together, these practices incubated proficiency steadily amid uncertainty. Lightweight experimentation surfaced insights economically while distributed knowledge reinforced communal progress. Reviews institutionalized recurrent strategizing responsive to change.

Netflix's commitment to trialing minimally yet frequently cultivated agility enabling nimbleness amid transition. Progress compounded through failing productively and learning lessons transparently.

Anthropic established reconstructive momentum by embracing risks benevolently. Distributing experiences transparently united cooperative efforts pragmatically. Institutionalizing reviews amplified strategic recalibration paced to disruption.

Together, these exemplars illuminated test-and-learn virtues: surfacing revelation economically, uniting understanding, and staging recurring strategizing. Success blossomed through cultivating many local experiments, extracting knowledge resiliently from failures, sharing experiences transparently and institutionalizing reviews.

Tracking multi-pronged experimentation, extracting understanding resiliently from setbacks and institutionalizing strategizing reconstructed proficiency steadily amid dynamical change.

Together, these practices nurtured capabilities enabling navigating disruption cooperatively and iteratively.

7.4 Embedding ongoing review and adaptation

Embedding recurrent reviews and adaptive pivoting cultivates strategic agility. Four practices reinforce these abilities: conducting retrospective analysis, adjusting plans iteratively, recalibrating collectively, documenting processes continually.

The following examines embedding ongoing review and adaptation through:
1. Conducting retrospective analysis
2. Adjusting plans iteratively
3. Recalibrating collectively
4. Documenting processes continually

Together, these practices instill reconstructive capacities enabling communities to navigate disruption cooperatively.

At Netflix, conducting retrospective analysis after each major initiative involved reviewing what succeeded and what lessons were learned. Outcome metrics were examined alongside qualitative feedback to understand both impacts and user sentiment. This process unearthed insights that could optimize future plans. By critically reflecting on strengths and weaknesses, the team cultivated an improvement-focused mindset.

Insights from retrospectives informed adjusting plans iteratively through subsequent sprints. Modifications addressed what wasn't working or could work better going forward. New hypotheses and tests were also developed based on analysis. This integrated review process allowed strategic direction to flexibly evolve incremental yet timely.

Anthropic engrained recalibration collectively by sharing analysis and planning adjustments widely across functions. Regular update meetings facilitated discussion around proposed changes before solidifying new direction. Diverse perspectives prompted deeper consideration of how strategy resonated with different areas. This fostered shared understanding and prevented detached decision making.

Documentation of processes at Netflix helped institutionalize methods for ongoing improvement. Guidelines ensured each project included defined review activities while historical analyses served as exemplars. Formal records supported continual refinement and on-boarding of practices over time and through personnel changes.

Together, these practices cultivated reconstructive reflexes attentive to fluctuation. Retrospective analysis surfaced rich insights, while iterative modification synchronized strategy with realities.

Collectively recalibrating strategies at Anthropic balanced collaboration with expediency. Distilling procedures institutionally amplified strategic versatility amid transition.

Embedded review and adaptation refreshed proficiency steadily at Netflix, guided by critical reflection and cooperative decision making. Strategies evolved timely through test-measure-learn iterations.

Together, these exemplars illuminated how continually nourished reconstructive capacities instill prowess navigating complexity and change. Success arose through retroactive evaluation, calibrated strategy integration, collective rationale and crystallized guidelines continually optimized.

By cultivating reflexive review and cooperative recalibration institutionally, these organizations cultivated agility amid turbulence. Strategic direction remained synchronized with realities identified retrospectively and distributed understanding united progress. Together, these reinforced reconstructive abilities enabling communities to thoughtfully steer through disruption.

Chapter **8**
Leading High-Performing Agile Teams

8.1 Self-organizing teams with shared leadership

Dispersing authority cultivates collaborative strength. Four practices reinforce self-organization: establishing autonomy supportively, distributing ownership equitably, coordinating flexibly, reviewing continuously.

The following examines self-organizing teams through:
1. Establishing autonomy supportively
2. Distributing ownership equitably
3. Coordinating flexibly
4. Reviewing continuously

Together, these practices nourish interdependence and adaptability amid change.

At Anthropic, teams established autonomy supportively through clearly defined yet permeable goals and processes. Management provided needed resources but avoided micromanaging work. This balance between structure and freedom cultivated intrinsic motivation.

Ownership of goals and tasks was distributed equitably based on members' interests, skills and availability rather than role or tenure. This flattened traditional hierarchies and engaged diversity. Collaboration became a member's primary responsibility.

To coordinate flexibly amid fluidity, daily stand-ups kept work visible and priorities aligned without imposing rigid workflows. Emerging alternatives could be discussed and adopted optimally.

Continuous review at weekly retrospectives allowed progress and interdependence to organically emerge through reflection. Challenges and enhancements were candidly reviewed to reinforce strengths and address weaknesses collectively.

This brought management and technical roles into parity, unifying efforts through shared purpose rather than directive control. Self-determination within clear yet permeable guardrails optimized engagement.

At Netflix, establishing autonomy through goal-focused yet non-prescriptive guidance cultivated initiative. This independence, balanced with support, energized innovation.

Distributing ownership equitably via transparent consultation ensured all talents informed prioritization. Interdependence replaced silos with shared victories.

Flexible coordination optimized expertise through fluid yet consistent alignment. Emergent cooperation addressed irregularities nimbly.

Continuous review united enhancement of strengths and addressing gaps cooperatively. Reflection strengthened interdependence steadily.

Together, dispersing authority reconstructed management as coaching, empowering self-synchronization. Teams prioritized purpose over procedure, cultivating shared prowess navigating uncertainty.

Self-organization instilled adaptability amid turbulence at Anthropic and Netflix through dispersed yet accountable rigs for harnessing diversity iteratively. Together, these practices furnished reconstructive dynamism enabling communities to cooperatively steer through disruption.

Anthropic and Netflix demonstrated how dispersing authority reconstructs roles relationally. Autonomy balanced with accountability cultivated proficiency willingly.

Equitable distribution of influence engaged diversity optimally. Interdependence replaced silos with shared understanding.

Flexible collaboration optimized fluid yet aligned cooperation. Emergence enriched proficiency amid irregularity.

Continuous reflection united purposefully addressing gaps to strengthen interdependence enduringly. Review invigorated reconstructive momentum cooperatively over time.

Together, these exemplars illuminated virtues of self-organization: cultivating initiative supportively within guardrails, engaging diversity readily, optimizing dynamism fluidly, and nourishing enhancement communally.

Success arose through dispersing stewardship liberally yet accountably, equitably engaging all, optimizing cooperation pliably, and reviewing reconstructively amid discontinuity. Together, these nourished interdependence and adaptability amid complexity.

By eschewing strict roles receptively yet retaining guidance resourcefully, Anthropic and Netflix furnished reconstructive strengths enabling teams to thoughtfully navigate turbulence cooperatively. Distributed authority seeded reconstruction through humanity.

8.2 Effective workflows, tools and technologies

Strategically adopting platforms cultivates collaborative agility. Four practices reinforce effective usage: selecting minimally yet robustly, integrating seamlessly, reviewing regularly, training continually.

The following examines reinforcing workflows through:

1. Selecting minimally yet robustly
2. Integrating seamlessly
3. Reviewing regularly
4. Training continually

Together, these practices nourish reconstructed strengths amid transition.

At Anthropic, selecting tools minimally yet robustly focused on streamlining workflows rather than featuring all options. Basic yet integral platforms like Slack and GitHub were optimized to maximize their collaborated affordances.

Integrating technologies seamlessly centralized coordination digitally to reduce friction. Well-integrated services prevented disjointed practices across tools. Users could fluidly access all collaboration and work-tracking functions.

Reviewing tool usage regularly involved candidly assessing what enhanced or hindered teamwork through short retrospectives. Feedback informed continuous refinements and potential additions or iterations.

Providing continual training supported tools being learned expressively according to evolving

needs. Just-in-time assistance cultivated independent proficiency over time. Reinforcement prevented expertise from being concentrated within early adopters.

This balanced strategic selection against feature bloat with optimal integration to cultivate reconstructed agility through technology. Regular review and learning further optimized function amid flux.

At Netflix, selecting basic tooling minimized distraction from core initiatives while robustly supporting constant experimentation.

Integrating services seamlessly across pipelines prevented interruption and reinforced coordination. Unified experiences strengthened collaboration fluidity.

Candid assessments at YouTube uncovered how technologies augmented or hindered progress. Insights optimized function and guided refinement.

Tailored guidance through internal documentation reinforced mastery pragmatically according to people's roles and projects over time. Recursive training continually reconstructed expertise.

Together, minimally disruptive selection, seamless integration, regular optimization and customized learning cultivated reconstructed agility amid turbulence. Tooling functioned transparently to cooperation rather than directing workstyles.

Strategic technologies furnished reconstructed strengths by streamlining coordination yet avoiding directive standardization. Regular review and contextual training updated supports timely. Together, these rendered tooling translucent and adaptively beneficial.

Anthropic, Netflix and YouTube exemplified reconstructing technological capacities strategically yet non-prescriptively.

Minimal yet integral selection optimized function while extensive options risked distraction. Streamlined robustness sufficed.

Seamless integration united digital spaces, strengthening continuity across partitioning. Frictionless-ness reinforced collaboration.

Regular reviews candidly assessed tool impacts, continually refining supports. Insights optimized reinforcement of strengths.

Customizable learning reconstructed self-reinforced mastery responsive to roles and projects incrementally. Guidance strengthened proficiency reconstructively over time.

Together, these reinforced tooling as augmentations cultivating collaborative agility resourcefully yet unobtrusively. Strategic selection, integration, review and training reconstructed technological capacities cooperatively.

Success arose through tools furnishing collaboration seamlessly yet unobtrusively. Regular optimization and contextual reinforcement continually updated supports reconstructively. Together, these practices furnished adaptive strengths navigating complexity through technology cooperatively.

8.3 Coaching agile mindsets and ways of working

Reconstructing perspectives cultivates cooperative strengths. Four practices reinforce agile mindsets: establishing growth-focused guidance supportively, normalizing experimentation positively, distributing accountability equitably, reviewing enhancement continuously.

The following examines cultivating agile mindsets through:
1. Establishing growth-focused guidance supportively
2. Normalizing experimentation positively
3. Distributing accountability equitably
4. Reviewing enhancement continuously

At Anthropic, establishing growth-focused guidance supportively involved coaching teams to view uncertainty as learning opportunities. Management discussions focused on skill-building rather than criticism so professionals felt motivated to challenge blindspots.
Normalizing experimentation positively reinforced trying innovations without judgment for failures. Teams understood setbacks as integral to the scientific process. Trying ideas allowed reconstructing understanding cooperatively through experience.

Distributing accountability equitably meant teams collectively owned outputs, preventing sole blameography. Outcomes reinforced interdependence rather than individualistic metrics. Together, cooperation strengthened greater than independence could.

Regular reviews critically assessed how encounters could reconstruct perspectives and practices cooperatively. Insights cultivated open-mindedness to alternative viewpoints and priorities emerging from experience. Non-attached consideration of diverse standpoints reinforced perspectives pliably.

Reinforcing reconstructed perspectives cooperatively cultivated proficiency navigating flux resiliently and resourcefully through humanity. Success arose from within, guided cooperatively.

At Netflix, growth-focused coaching reconstructed setbacks as lessons instilling perseverance. Professionals embraced uncertainty intrinsically as an opportunity to reinforce strengths cooperatively.

Experimentation was normalized by regarding alternatives thoughtfully rather than rejecting ideas prematurely. Hypotheses informed progress through democratic consideration.

Equitable ownership of outcomes cultivated peer accountability efficiently. Interdependence replaced silos with shared understanding of collective responsibilities.

Continuous reflection at retrospectives optimized learning from diverse viewpoints and priorities emerging from experiences. Reconstruction reinforced pliability and community cooperatively over time.

Together, reconstructing mindsets through guidance, experimentation, distributed responsibility and review cultivated adaptive strengths navigating irregularity skillfully yet non-attached. Success arose inwardly, then outwardly through humanity.

Strategies furnished reconstructed dynamism amid discontinuity by cultivating proficiency to cooperatively: view uncertainty resourcefully, hypothesize collaboratively, own interdependence, and reflect reconstructively. Perspectives flexibly navigated complexity through humanity.

Anthropic, Netflix, and other pioneers exemplified reconstructing perspectives supportively.

Growth-focused coaching instilled perseverance in facing uncertainty resiliently as a community. Professionals embraced irregularity intrinsically.

Normalizing experimentation regarded alternatives thoughtfully through democratic consideration. Hypotheses informed progress cooperatively.

Equitable accountability dispensed blame, cultivating peer ownership of interdependence. Silos gave way to shared understanding.

Continuous reflection optimized emergent insights, flexibly updating viewpoints and priorities over time. Reconstruction unified diversity reconstructively.

Together, this cultivated aptitude navigating disruption skillfully yet objectively. Success arose inwardly then outwardly through cooperation.

Strategies furnished reconstructive strengths amid discontinuity by: embracing uncertainty resourcefully, hypothesizing collaboratively, owning interdependence, and reflecting pliably. Perspectives navigated complexity smoothly through shared understanding.

Regular optimization of mindsets through guidance, experimentation, responsibility and review rendered proficiency adaptable. Reconstruction occurred cooperatively from within, empowering outward progression.

0.4 Facilitating team autonomy and accountability

At Anthropic, cultivating reconstructed autonomy began by establishing supportive guidance to empower initiative while preventing disconnect. Leadership focused on cultivating intrinsic motivation through open advice and resource allocation aligned with team objectives.

Distributing ownership equitably involved teams directly prioritizing work and accounting for outputs cooperatively. Interdependence replaced reliance on directives from above with self-management balanced by shared responsibility.

Regular reviews involved candid reflection on experiences from all perspectives to strengthen future collaboration. Peer accountability reconstructed understanding of collective challenges and opportunities for enhanced coordination.

Continual reinforcement of interdependence over independence optimized orientation around shared goals.

Outcomes reinforced the importance of flexibility and community to navigate complexity successfully long-term.

By balancing independence with interdependence transparently, these strategies nourished proficiency navigating uncertainty resourcefully through reconstructing empowerment and responsibility cooperatively. Success arose inwardly then outwardly through unity.

At Netflix, establishing supportive guidance focused on cultivating self-reliance through open advice and empowering teams with flexibility. Leadership coached autonomy accountably rather than dictated tasks.

Distributing ownership equitably involved directly prioritizing work and collectively accounting for results transparently. Interdependence replaced reliance on directives with reconstructed coordination.

Regular peer reviews candidly shared perspectives to strengthen future collaboration. Collective reflection optimized understanding challenges and opportunities to enhance cooperation moving forward.

Reinforcement of interdependence over sole independence-oriented efforts around shared goals cooperatively. Outcomes emphasized reconstructing flexibility and community successfully over the long term.

Together, practices struck a balance fostering independence complemented responsibly by interdependence. Strategies nourished proficiency navigating irregularity resiliently through reconstructing empowerment and responsibility cooperatively from within.

Strategic cultivation of empowered yet accountable autonomy furnished strengths amid complexity. Reconstructed guidance, equitable delegation and regular optimization of understanding cultivated adapted proficiency navigation disruption cooperatively resourcefully.

Anthropic, Netflix and other innovators exemplified reconstructing autonomy accountably through guidance, ownership and review.

Supportive coaching focused on cultivating self-reliance and flexibility cooperatively over directives. Leadership emphasized intrinsic motivation.

Distributed prioritization and transparency replaced reliance on directives with reconstructed coordination. Interdependence strengthened management.

Regular reflection optimized future collaboration through sharing diverse perspectives candidly. Collective assessment updated cooperative practices.

Reinforcement of interdependence-oriented efforts cooperatively around shared goals successfully long term. Flexibility complemented responsibility transparently.

Together, practices balanced empowerment with interdependence fluidly. Strategies nourished resilience facing irregularity through reconstructing direction and responsibility collaboratively from within.

Reconstruction occurred inwardly then outwardly through a framework cultivating autonomy accountably. Flexible practices furnished strengths navigating complexity cooperatively through humanity. Guidance, delegation and reflection cultivated adaptive proficiency resourcefully.

Chapter 9
Enabling Agility through Structure and Process

9.1 Fluid, modular organizational designs

Anthropic established flexible coordinates purposefully by regularly reconsidering alignments responsive to evolving goals and capabilities. Dynamic structuring optimized coordination through minimally necessary integration.

Functions were distributed modularly into interdependent yet independent cells minimizing interlinkages. Teams prioritized missions autonomously while reinforcing communal success through open collaboration.

Services were integrated transparently utilizing lightweight standards at semipermeable interphases. Interdependence replaced siloed redundancies with modular access bolstering agility.

Regular iterative review reconstructed understanding of interconnections to weaken rigidity. Insights cultivated reconstructing organizational design pliably in response to emerging conditions cooperatively over the long term.

By balancing independence with interdependence nimbly, these strategies nourished navigating ambiguity resiliently through reconstructing frames, divisions and associations cooperatively. Proficiency arose from within, guided resourcefully.

At Netflix, flexible coordinates were established purposefully through regular reconsideration of alignments responsive to flux. Dynamic structuring optimized coordination with minimal necessary integration.

Functions were distributed modularly into autonomous yet cooperating cells with minimized interlinkages. Teams prioritized missions autonomously while reinforcing shared success openly.

Services were integrated transparently using lightweight standards at porous interphases. Interdependence replaced siloed redundancies pliably with modular access bolstering dexterity.

Iterative reviews reconstructed understanding of interconnections to dilute rigidity progressively. Insights cultivated reconstructing designs pliably over the long term in response to emerging conditions cooperatively.

Together, practices balanced autonomy and interdependence deftly. Strategies nourished navigating irregularity resiliently through reconstructing frames, divisions and associations cooperatively from within. Adaptive proficiency emerged resourcefully.

Strategic cultivation of modular designs furnished strengths amid discontinuity. Reconstruction occurred transparently through a framework optimizing coordination yet flexibility, teams yet community, independence yet interdependence deftly.
Anthropic, Netflix and other innovators exemplified reconstructing structures modularly through purposeful realignment, functional distribution and iterative review.

Flexible coordinates were established responsively through regular reconsideration aligned with flux. Dynamic structuring optimized synergistic independence and interdependence.

Missions were prioritized autonomously in distributed functions with minimized interlinkages. Teams reinforced shared prosperity through candid collaboration.

Services integrated translucently at porous divisions utilizing lightweight standards. Interdependence complemented specialty resiliently with reconstructive engagement.

Regular reconstructive assessments diluted ossification, cultivating design adaptability aligned with emerging prospects cooperatively over the long term.

Together, practices delicately balanced autonomy and community. Strategies nourished navigating irregularity capably through reconstructing frames, departments and affiliations cooperatively from within.

Strategic development furnished strengths facing discontinuity by optimizing: synergy amid independence, specialization amid generality, and plasticity amid permanence transparently through iterative reconfiguration. Reconstruction occurred resourcefully.

9.2 Adaptable policies, protocols and job roles

Anthropic established reconstructive protocols transparently by regularly reassessing alignments responsive to evolving requirements and talents. Dynamic guidelines optimized coordination through judicious reconstruction.

Roles were distributed iteratively utilizing lightweight standards for rotational specialization. Individuals reinforced communal success through open collaboration and career reconstruction.

Enhancements were integrated communally at porous divisions utilizing iterative procedures. Interdependence replaced rigid constraints with flexible access bolstering nimbleness.

Continuous reviewing reconstructed understanding of interdependencies to dilute rigidity progressively. Insights cultivated adaptively reconstructing frameworks cooperatively aligned with emerging conditions.

By balancing independence with interdependence deftly, these strategies nourished navigating irregularity resiliently through reconstructing boundaries, assignments and progressions cooperatively. Proficiency arose resourcefully.

At Netflix, reconstructive protocols were established transparently through regular reassessment responsive to flux. Dynamic guidelines optimized synergy amid specialties.

Roles were distributed iteratively utilizing lightweight standards for rotational specialization. Individuals reinforced shared success openly through career reconstruction collaboratively.

Enhancements integrated communally at porous divisions utilizing iterative procedures. Interdependence complemented skills pliably through reconstructive engagement.

Continuous reviews reconstituted understanding of interconnections to weaken solidification adaptively. Insights cultivated frameworks pliably aligned with emerging prospects cooperatively.

Together, practices nimbly balanced independence and community. Strategies nourished navigating turbulence capably through reconstructing boundaries, roles and progressions cooperatively from within.

Strategic development furnished strengths facing irregularity by optimizing flexibility amid permanence transparently through iterative reconstitution. Reconstruction transpired resourcefully.

Anthropic, Netflix and other innovators exemplified reconstructing frameworks iteratively through transparent realignment, rotational distribution and continuous review.

Reconstructive protocols were established responsively through regular reassessment responsive to flux. Dynamic guidelines optimized interdependence and independence dexterously.

Roles were prioritized autonomously in distributed functions utilizing lightweight standards for specialization and career plasticity. Individuals reinforced shared prosperity openly.

Enhancements integrated transparently at porous divisions through iterative processes. Interdependence complemented expertise resiliently with reconstructive engagement.

Sustained reconstructive assessments diluted rigidification progressively, cultivating framework adaptability aligned with emerging prospects cooperatively over time.

Together, practices subtly balanced autonomy and community. Strategies nourished navigating irregularity adeptly through reconstructing boundaries, roles and progressions cooperatively from within.

Strategic development furnished strengths facing discontinuity by optimizing synergy amid independence, specialization amid collaboration, and plasticity amid permanence openly through continuous reconstitution.

9.3 Seamless horizontal and cross-silo collaboration

Reconstructing linkages cooperatively cultivates fluidity amid flux. Four practices reinforce reconstructed connections: establishing reconstructive interphases transparently, distributing collaborations iteratively, integrating insights communally, reviewing networks continuously.

Anthropic established reconstructive interphases transparently by regularly reassessing alignments responsive to evolving synergies. Dynamic guidelines optimized coordination through judicious reconstruction. Associated divisions oriented autonomously yet collaboratively.

Connections were distributed iteratively utilizing lightweight standards. Individuals reinforced communal success through open collaboration and reconstructive engagements. Insights arose laterally amid rotating partnerships resiliently navigating irregularity.

Understandings were integrated communally at porous divisions utilizing iterative processes. Interdependence replaced rigid silos with flexible interchange bolstering proficiency. Associated domains oriented independently yet interdependently.

Continuous reviewing reconstituted appreciation of interrelationships to weaken solidification adaptively. Lessons cultivated reconstructing linkages cooperatively aligned with emerging prospects. Associated divisions oriented independently yet interdependently.

At Netflix, reconstructive interphases were established transparently through regular reassessment responsive to dynamic synergies. Guidelines optimized coordination amid independent yet interwoven domains.

Collaborations were distributed iteratively utilizing lightweight standards. Individuals reinforced shared achievement openly through reconstructive engaging. Insights arose laterally amid rotational alliances resiliently navigating irregularity.

Understandings integrated transparently at porous divisions through iterative processes. Interdependence complemented skills pliably through reconstructive interchange. Associated specialties oriented autonomously yet interdependently.

Sustained reconstructive assessments diluted rigidification progressively, cultivating linkage reconstitution aligned with emerging prospects cooperatively. Domains oriented independently yet interdependently.

Together, practices subtly balanced independence and interdependence. Strategies nourished navigating ambiguity adeptly through reconstructing intersections, partnerships and affiliations collaboratively from within.

Strategic development furnished strengths facing discontinuity by optimizing flexibility amid permanence transparently through continuous reconstitution. Reconstruction transpired resourcefully.
Anthropic, Netflix and others exemplified reconstructing linkages iteratively through transparent realignment, rotational collaboration and continuous review.
Reconstructive interphases were established responsively through regular reassessment aligned with dynamic synergies. Guidelines optimized interdependence and independence deftly.

Collaborations were prioritized autonomously in distributed domains utilizing lightweight standards. Individuals reinforced shared prosperity openly.

Insights integrated translucently at porous divisions through iterative processes. Interdependence complemented skills resiliently with reconstructive interchange.

Enduring reconstructive assessments diluted rigidity progressively, cultivating framework plasticity aligned with emerging prospects cooperatively over time. Domains oriented independently yet interdependently.

Together, practices nimbly balanced independence and community. Strategies nourished navigating ambiguity capably through reconstructing intersections, alliances and affiliations cooperatively from within.

Strategic development furnished strengths facing discontinuity by optimizing flexibility amid stability transparently through continuous reconstitution. Reconstruction transpired beneficially.

9.4 Continuous improvement of agile capabilities

Reconstructing proficiency collaboratively cultivates augmentation amid flux. Four practices reinforce enhanced abilities: establishing reconstructive enhancement transparently, distributing advancements iteratively, integrating improvements communally, reviewing aptitude continuously.

Anthropic established reconstructive enhancement transparently by regularly reassessing requirements and evolving talents. Dynamic approaches optimized faculty through judicious reconstruction.

Advancements were distributed iteratively utilizing interconnectivity. Individuals reinforced communal growth through open collaboration and reconstructive learning.

Improvements were integrated communally at porous divisions utilizing iterative processes. Interdependence replaced constraints with flexible aptitude bolstering proficiency.

Continuous reviewing reconstituted awareness of interdependencies to dilute rigidity progressively. Insights cultivated reconstructing proficiencies cooperatively aligned with emerging conditions.

Together, these strategies nourished navigating irregularity resiliently through reconstructing knowledge, approaches and refinement cooperatively from within outwardly. Augmentation transpired resourcefully.

At Netflix, reconstructive enhancement was established transparently through regular reassessment responsive to evolving demands and skills. Dynamic methodologies optimized expertise through judicious reconstitution.

Advancements were distributed iteratively using lightweight interconnection. Individuals reinforced shared development openly through reconstructive coaching. Improvements integrated transvirantly at porous divisions via iterative processes. Interdependence supplemented talents adaptably through reconstructive engagement.

Continuous reviews reconstituted appreciation of interrelationships to dilute solidification progressively, cultivating framework plasticity aligned with emerging prospects cooperatively.

Collectively, practices delicately balanced autonomy and interdependence. Strategies nourished navigating irregularity capably through reconstructing learnings, tactics and refinement cooperatively from within.

Reinvention occurred resourcefully. Reconstruction furnished strengths facing discontinuity by optimizing proficiency amid permanence transparently through continuous reconstitution. Anthropic, Netflix and others exemplified reconstructing abilities iteratively through transparent realignment, rotational advancement and continuous review.

Reconstructive enhancement was established responsively through regular reassessment aligned with evolving demands and skills. Methodologies optimized expertise deftly.

Advancements were prioritized autonomously in distributed domains using lightweight interconnection. Individuals reinforced shared growth openly.
Improvements integrated translucently at porous divisions via iterative processes. Interdependence complemented talents resiliently with reconstructive engagement.

Enduring reconstructive assessments diluted rigidity progressively, cultivating framework plasticity aligned with emerging prospects cooperatively over time.

Together, practices deftly balanced autonomy and community. Strategies nourished navigating ambiguity capably through reconstructing learnings, tactics and refinement cooperatively from within.

Strategic development furnished strengths facing discontinuity by optimizing flexibility amid stability transparently through continuous reconstitution. Reconstruction transpired beneficially.

Synopsis

In this dynamic book, the author explores the principles of agile leadership and how they can be applied to navigate change and uncertainty in the modern business landscape. Through real-world examples and practical tips, readers will discover how to embrace agility, adapt quickly to changing circumstances, and foster a culture of innovation and resilience within their teams. This book offers valuable insights and strategies for leaders to thrive in an ever-evolving and fast-paced environment.

About the Author

Mustafa A. Nejem is a maritime visionary with a captain's heart and an island soul. In his island home, the sea's love, sailing's legacy, and leadership's flame passed down through generations with pride and glory. He is a skilled navigator of words, charting a course through the vast ocean of knowledge. With his expertise and passion, he guides readers towards prosperous shores, unveiling the secrets of maritime life and business success in concise and captivating prose.

www.ingramcontent.com/pod-product-compliance
Lightning Source LLC
Chambersburg PA
CBHW080851120626
46546CB00008B/2786